Vergil

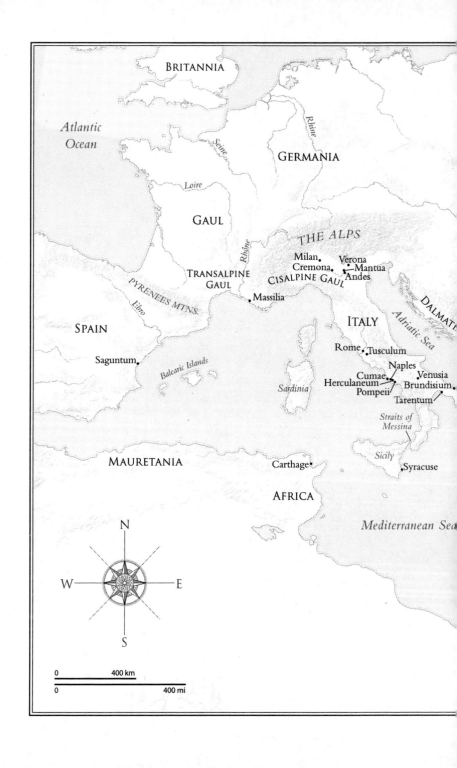

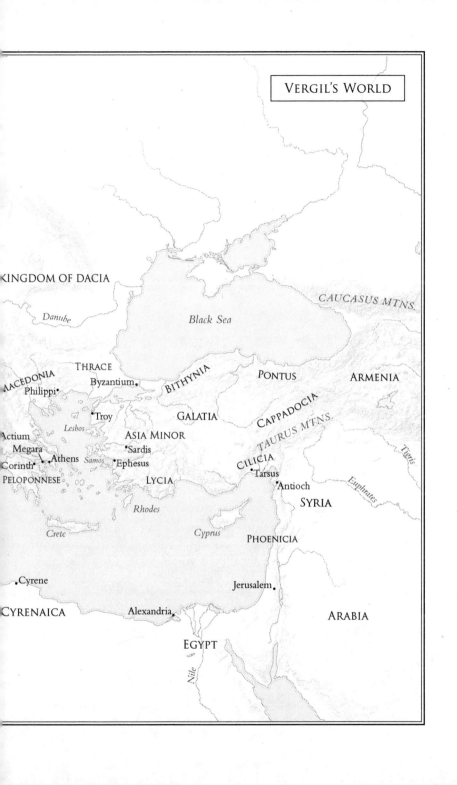

VERGIL'S WORLD

KINGDOM OF DACIA

Danube

Black Sea

CAUCASUS MTNS.

THRACE

MACEDONIA
Philippi•

Byzantium•

BITHYNIA

PONTUS

ARMENIA

•Troy

Lesbos

GALATIA

CAPPADOCIA

TAURUS MTNS.

Actium

ASIA MINOR

Megara

•Sardis

CILICIA

Corinth•
Athens   Samos   •Ephesus

•Tarsus

Tigris

PELOPONNESE

LYCIA

•Antioch

Euphrates

Rhodes

SYRIA

Crete

Cyprus

PHOENICIA

•Cyrene

Jerusalem•

CYRENAICA

Alexandria•

ARABIA

EGYPT

Nile

Vergil

The Poet's Life

Sarah Ruden

· ANCIENT LIVES ·

Yale

UNIVERSITY PRESS

NEW HAVEN & LONDON

Published with assistance from the foundation established in memory of
Amasa Stone Mather of the Class of 1907, Yale College.

Yale University Press books may be purchased in quantity for
educational, business, or promotional use. For information, please e-mail
sales.press@yale.edu (U.S. office) or sales@yaleup.co.uk (U.K. office).

Frontispiece: Beehive Mapping.

Set in the Yale typeface designed by Matthew Carter, and Louize,
designed by Matthieu Cortat, by Integrated Publishing Solutions.
Printed in the United States of America.

Library of Congress Control Number: 2022950366
ISBN 978-0-300-25661-1 (hardcover: alk. paper)
ISBN 978-0-300-28200-9 (paperback)

A catalogue record for this book is available from the British Library.

10 9 8 7 6 5 4 3 2 1

· ANCIENT LIVES ·

Ancient Lives unfolds the stories of thinkers, writers, kings, queens, conquerors, and politicians from all parts of the ancient world. Readers will come to know these figures in fully human dimensions, complete with foibles and flaws, and will see that the issues they faced—political conflicts, constraints based in gender or race, tensions between the private and public self—have changed very little over the course of millennia.

James Romm
Series Editor

For the bees

Muse, tell me why. What stung the queen of heaven,
What insult to her power made her drive
This righteous hero through so much undoing
And suffering? Can gods' hearts know such fury?

(Vergil, *Aeneid* 1.8–11)

Contents

Preface

This book follows on my efforts to convey in English the tenderness and majesty of Vergil's poetry. In my late teens, I was recruited for Classics by reading the first work definitely ascribed to Vergil, the pastoral *Eclogues,* and my harebrained undergraduate version of four of those ten poems brought enough support and encouragement to put me on the path toward professional translation. Many years later, in 2008, Yale University Press published my complete English *Aeneid,* and in 2021 an extensively revised second edition of it, for which I have Susanna Braund's expert editorial supervision and unstinting encouragement to thank. *Aeneid* quotations in this book are from the 2021 translation.

I have always been proud of my relationship with "my" authors. They seem to become living presences as I dig in the text's details for evidence of their moods and visions. I rely on what they "tell me" even when that means resisting conventional English renderings, which I often see applied to a great variety of authors and genres in a mechanical, classroom-translation way. But this attitude threatened me with a tragic level of hubris as I began to research and write about Vergil's actual life.

How could I describe it, after all? The man was like Shakespeare in being hard to know in proportion to his greatness; like Shakespeare, he disappeared into his writing, so that the breadth, flexibility, and imagination of the results make the process seem uncanny. How could any mere life produce such beauty? After much hesitation, I set off on a quest to know Vergil the man better through what *probably* follows from such things as his physical, social, and literary contexts and his own literary innovations.

I now find myself greatly indebted to the cumulative findings of experts in philology, ancient history, and archaeology; but especially to Susanna Braund in her capacity as the leading exponent of Vergil's reception. It has been a sobering corrective to learn more about what became of Vergil's persona in the millennia after his death, though that is not the subject of this book. Special thanks are also due to the eminent social and literary historian of imperial Rome, John Bodel. But this volume is indebted for its very existence to the editors James Romm and Heather Gold, and to my agent Gail Hochman.

Vergil

Introduction

THINKING BACK TOWARD
THE REAL VERGIL

G reat works of literature are sly and powerful beasts who pounce on readers, grabbing them by the neck and shaking them back and forth. The young Augustine looks like a typical victim of Vergil's *Aeneid*. The schoolboy being brought up Christian in fourth-century CE North Africa found the first-century BCE epic poem of pagan Rome the most impressive thing in his cultural life to date. Tellingly, his reaction shows no interest in the poem's theme of individual sacrifice in the name of imperial destiny; rather, into middle age he remembered weeping for Dido, the hero Aeneas' lover who is abandoned and commits suicide (*Confessions* 1.20–21). And though the great theologian and founder of institutional Catholic monasticism could not admit it, those scenes never ceased to touch him.

One problem generated by such reactions is how to view the author's life. A literary work of great endurance to which a particular era gives rise is not fundamentally about that era but more about the nature of experience. And the author's insights into experience come in such appealing forms that many readers take him (or her) for a sort of companion and adherent.

Vergil's greatest poem, the *Aeneid,* is obtrusively "about" the establishment, accomplished at high cost, of the Roman nation through the providential survival and triumph of the first Roman emperor Augustus' refugee ancestor Aeneas; and Vergil's two other major works, the *Eclogues* and the *Georgics,* in some ways prepare for this topic. But like Jane Austen's anxious love of England during the Napoleonic era, Vergil's demonstrated attitude toward the most important public events of his lifetime – a long series of civil wars and the accession of a virtual autocrat – is, in itself, in no way original or compelling. Brooding patriotism, execration of civil war, celebration of the new regime, and similar dated moods and assertions that have sometimes taken center stage in studies of Vergil can be more detailed and explicit in other authors of the time in whom we have far less natural interest. As always, there has to be something about the *author himself* that is vital to that thing called literary achievement, some reason *he* brought into being something so communicative and congenial.

This reality is at the root of the kind of open-ended biographical problems Hermione Lee samples in her collection of essays *Virginia Woolf's Nose.* Lee demonstrates how, with their intense personal investment in a particular author, pursuers of that author's life make up details they cannot find in their research and overinterpret what they do find.

And this is the treatment given to relatively fresh evidence in our age of secure archives, high scholarly standards, and keen competition among biographers. For Vergil, who lived from 70 to 19 BCE, the biographical tradition veered out of control from the first and never corrected itself. In the ancient world, rumor, folklore, prejudice, whimsy, and inference from fictional works were habitual sources for biographical "fact." The Athenian tragedian Euripides, a legend states, was torn to pieces in the woods by hunting dogs belonging to his patron, the king of semi-wild Macedonia. The literary inspiration for this story might be the dismemberment of his protagonist Pentheus at the hands of feral women in the *Bacchae,* or the fatal dragging of his Hippolytus by spooked horses in the play named for him, though Euripides' unpopularity in his native Athens no doubt helped the story along.

But Vergil presents an acute biographical case. We know a great deal less about him personally than about the second most important poet in the Augustan literary circle, Horace; Vergil not only was a private man by preference, he also seems to have evoked — no doubt with the help of powerful imperial patronage — a most un-Roman respect for his privacy. Since then, Vergil's distance and blurriness as a human being have enticed people to read his life and his thinking so as best to suit their own lives and their own thinking.

The consequent distortions go far beyond the political. Through the long period of Late Antiquity and far beyond, the *Aeneid* was a school text. For centuries, it was mined for oratorical fuel, and passages were assigned for transformation into prating hackwork — though the author was, on all the evidence, the quintessential anti-orator, who rejected both the conventional training and the conventional career and lived and created in intense inwardness. The classroom presentation of Vergil's work was nearly always moralistic, setting up the hero Aeneas — a sooty and worn but unbending ramrod of a divine destiny (a destiny several other characters plausibly doubt) — as a model for little boys and teenagers. As to language, Vergil's Latin is inimitably beautiful but in some ways idiosyncratic. His style provoked attacks in his own time yet was later emulated. Such emulation gave untold stimulus to later literature but hardly improved the sense of Vergil as a human being who struggled to develop his gifts, someone whose life as well as his work could inspire readers and writers.

Also in the classroom, the natural science, geography, history, myth, and legend that blend so vividly and tellingly in the sweep of his scene painting and narration were reduced to isolated facts for memorization and thereby leached of interest. But Vergil was anything but a dry scholar; he was an opportunistic borrower and probably an ebullient innovator, expanding a certain quantity of old material with great verve and inventing whatever else he felt he needed. (The poor survival of earlier literature prevents us from drawing a line between the two activities.) Yet the influence of the invented world he shows us doubles back absurdly to suggest that he was an omniscient, godlike creator. A senior professor at Harvard, in the bliss of connecting a line of Vergil to an obscure source, chirped, "Vergil knew everything." I had become a Vergil fan largely on my own, but if I had not, I would have absorbed from my instructors that both studying and worshipping Vergil were chores. The thought of simply reading him, and liking what he wrote, and wondering about his day-to-day life would not have occurred to me.

Any serious reconsideration of the life requires a skeptical look at the pedantic angle. Because too much could never possibly be learned about all things Vergilian, biographical material as well — collected and elaborated from earlier accounts — eventually found its way into enormous compendia of Late Antique Vergil study notes. This was not a standard environment for biography in the ancient world. Information about authors' lives might be added to texts of their work, as in modern introductions. Freestanding biographies honored great men and illustrated political and moral principles or enabled character or historical analysis. The anonymous biographers and other authors including Xenophon, Sallust, Tacitus, and Plutarch came nowhere near modern standards of accuracy or balance, but they did manifest the basic virtue of writing about real individuals as such and trying to connect their private and inner lives to things they did.

Suetonius, the first extant Vergil biographer, who was active in the late first and early second centuries CE, fits more or less into this category. His Life of Vergil (thought to depend on an account by Varius, who was a member of Vergil's circle and had access to his documents) does not stand out sharply (despite an eccentric manuscript history) from other Suetonian authors' lives. True, Vergil is given a blessed birth, but it is typical for such mythologizing to creep in concerning an important man.

By the fourth century, however, the Life appearing under the name Donatus (a scholar and teacher) had become a function of Vergil worship. Narrative influenced by the Bible has seeped in, and Vergil appears like Joseph to Pharaoh: a divinely gifted husbandman and prophetic counselor to the emperor Augustus. Later biography even wandered into verse, as if completing a circle back to Vergil's own calling of fictive artistry.

An authoritative and yet almost oblivious mode of depicting Vergil thus took root, which was convenient for a variety of strange purposes. Vergil's fourth eclogue was said to predict the birth of Christ. (Almost certainly it predicted the peacemaking birth of a son — the baby turned out to be a girl — to Mark Antony and Octavia, sister to Octavian, the man who became Vergil's patron some years before securing unchallenged rule and assuming the title Augustus.) Vergil is the guide for Dante's persona in the *Inferno* and the *Purgatorio;* the Roman poet knows everything that matters about the universe, human history, and the divine will. He must stop short of paradise because he died before the requisite religious faith existed. But his exemplary role in revered ancient Roman civilization, and what certain Christian thinkers styled "pagan virtue," made him an ideal mentor for a Christian. Let me be completely clear, however: the living Vergil was an ordinary, functional pagan; the only alternative in his time and environment would have been conversion to Judaism.

The puppetlike nature of the Vergil persona lent itself to further nonsense in later eras. Vergil has been presented as a suitable apologist for empire in its modern Western style; he has also been touted as a sly anti-imperialist. But in *Aeneid* 5.282–285 (and there is a wealth of similar evidence), a young slave woman, a skilled weaver who is nursing twins, figures among the prizes in the pious and patriotic funeral games. Is she a war captive? Did her captor sire her children? How does she feel about her situation? What is her future? *We* care, *we* wonder, but the poet obviously does not; it is his story, with his themes, not ours. The same goes for the anti-totalitarian and anti–Vietnam War Vergils of a few decades ago and the queer Vergil of today. Such activist readings have to presume coded protests that only people at a mammoth cultural, political, and linguistic distance from the author can decipher. We need to make our own peace with our own histories and leave Vergil out of them.

How, then, do we look more clearly at Vergil himself? An account of how his environment as a whole could have worked on him promises help. How might his class, ethnic, and geographical backgrounds have shaped him? What kind of family relations, education, love life, and friendships would have awaited him? What did poor health mean in his historical context? How did authors of his time think differently from us about language and literature, society and governance, nature and culture? And how might the lives and careers of Vergil's patrons and the rest of his coterie have helped form his own life and career?

An excellent model for how to make such facts and probabilities enliven skimpy data is Stephen Greenblatt's *Will in the World*, about the life of Shakespeare. I emulate Greenblatt's approach by stressing Vergil's development as a writer specifically and examining how that role fit (or didn't) into his life as a son, student, protégé, and so on. But this takes a literary biographer only so far. The most important moments in most authors' lives are those of quiet work, and they themselves may not even suspect the real mechanisms of their breakthroughs. Biographers tend to concentrate on relationships, those loud, visible moving parts of any life, and it took the generally insulting attitude of Sylvia Plath biography (which tended to grade her performance as a daughter, girlfriend, object of charity, friend, wife, mother, and hostess) to shake the genre into better sense: a writer—even a subordinate and dependent person like Plath or Vergil—is first and foremost a writer.

What hope, then, does a biographer have of looking within at what is most important? This scrutiny seems to require a degree of psychologizing, and what I mean by that is only the effort to make closer connections than previously between things that happen on the page and things that happened in reality. I reject the sneer "amateur psychology" this effort may provoke. When I look at the ups and downs of professional psychology since its inception and at the adept amateur psychology that good authors model—not to mention the instinctive psychologizing that makes ordinary life possible—I wonder whether I should ever hold back cautious guesses about mood and motivation.

But there is one big trap here, which Greenblatt respects. Though much that Shakespeare—and Vergil, and other authors of equal éclat—experienced must have been stressful, little of it was unusual.

The ways they processed it through language *were* unusual but also included enough of the common touch that the words come across as emblematic. How does this happen? The actual "process," that great object of audiences' curiosity (is it supposed to be an equation, with circumstances and actions, talents and character as inputs, and a given kind of book as the output?), must amount to a powerful secret even in the case of far less secretive authors.

The trick to dealing with this powerful secret in Vergil's case is, I believe, to concentrate on the power in order to diminish the secrecy. Influential authors do influential literary work—a tautology, of course, but prod it a little, and it yields a more useful formulation: literary work is not only what these authors do but also who they are. Their subtlety and adaptability in respect to their work can be inferred not only from their pages but from their lives. Seemingly private things they seek or avoid (employment, marriage, children, travel, friendships, a certain kind of home or friends or clothes or manners) tend to be connected to their hope to impress the world permanently and publicly with their words. Writers game their lives out for literary purposes, or they are out of the game before we have a chance of knowing anything about them.

Vergil, with such conspicuous negatives for his time and class (no wife, no children, no settled home, extreme reserve, a chief patron he pushed to the edge of his tolerance for delay), looks very good at this gamesmanship. In that sense he would have been the first truly modern author, an extraordinary individual whose work swallows up his identity: "genius," "prodigy," "phenomenon," "obsessive," and similar terms indicate the distance from the ordinary and expected. This was not at all the usual writerly persona in the ancient world, where civic and professional duty and public performance in an authoritative forum tended to define literary roles. Even a star like Plato, Cicero, or Horace appears anxious to depict his own literary achievement as situated among or fostered by others. Vergil started as they did, on the evidence of the chummier *Eclogues*. But so different was his mature mood that on his deathbed he defied the regime that had made him rich and famous: he demanded that the draft of the *Aeneid* be destroyed because he had not polished it to his satisfaction.

As a translator of Vergil, and the first one to produce a line-by-line, tightly metrical rendering of the *Aeneid*, which required sweating over certain lines for hours, and then sweating over thousands of revisions for the second edition, I probably know better than anyone alive how it feels to spend time as he reportedly did. There are worse foundations for writing about his life.

To build on this foundation, I am going to use a new kind of evidence, modern literary biography. The great modern authors seem to have much in common: a failed or shunned conventional career or other social role, an energetic but eccentric and long-drawn-out apprenticeship, bad or merely writing-centered romantic and domestic behavior, escape from the usual demands on time through illness or travel or deracination or social withdrawal. Naturally there are exceptions, but a rough accounting of what separates authors, or at least modern authors, as a group from other people is that very thing, separation, the drawing back of the self into the mind. This is one trait consistently attributed to and evident in Vergil. Is he not, to some degree, knowable from the behavior of his descendants?

Luckily for my inspiration and encouragement, we are living in a golden age of literary biography. If the more careful, more balanced treatment of the most prominent authors' lives reveals one thing, it is that these authors are dizzyingly different from us, but more knowable if we repress our envious condescension and concede that they knew what they were doing. Many things about Vergil's life made more sense to me once I dared to grasp that this shy young man from nowhere, who struggled from line to line as he composed and revised, sensed in some part of his mind that if he tried hard enough he could cause the world to welcome millions of copies of his work, whereas just a few thousand copies of his patron the first Roman emperor's sole extant composition (if he did write it himself), *The Achievements of the Divine Augustus,* would ever circulate, and only for scholarly purposes. It seems very wrong to ignore the real, living passion through which Vergil testified to the transcendence of the mind and spirit over material power.

CHAPTER ONE

Origins

The earliest surviving biography of Vergil, composed by Suetonius and probably including among its sources direct testimony to the life that had ended more than a century earlier, begins this way:

> Publius Vergilius Maro, who was born in Mantua, had parents with lower-class backgrounds. This was the case for his father in particular, who some people claim was a potter, although the consensus is that he started out as the employee of someone called Magus, an official who assured attendance in court; became his son-in-law later on due to his hard work; and added significantly to his small amount of property by buying up woods and cultivating bees. Vergil was born during the first consulship of Gnaeus Pompeius the Great and Marcus Licinius Crassus, on the Ides of October [October 15 of the year 70 BCE], in a district named Andes, not far from Mantua. (The Life of Vergil 1–2)

How can we understand, expand on, and extrapolate from this passage? It is important in grounding the poet in ways the story of his later life seldom does. This account gives basic information on his family and its social and economic rise, and names a precise birthdate and locale. During Vergil's adult life, a phase when almost all famous authors are personally better known to posterity, he largely disappears into his work and his work's fame. He leaves no letters to or from himself, nor any other personal documents of any kind unless a tomb inscription of doubtful authenticity counts — and it provides only the barest outline of his life, adding nothing to what is offered by other sources. (Shakespeare's epitaph comes to mind, with its not very exciting "Do Not Disturb" verse message.) In his indisputably genuine literary work, the "I" is sparse and includes little that is personally revealing. Early on he does write in warm, sometimes exuberant tones of members of two broadly overlapping groups: poets whose work has not survived (or has survived only in disappointing fragments) and political players connected to the man who became the first Roman emperor, Octavian, later called Augustus. But contextualized readings of these passages (see Chapter 4) leave me wondering how many friends, confidants, and colleagues he saw in the two groups, and how many competitors and handlers. The poet Horace, a hyper-talented freedman's son who lived on imperial patronage himself, tells in *Satires* 1.5.39–44 of meeting Vergil with the embraces of devoted friendship, but there is no clear sign that Vergil reciprocated Horace's feelings. Vergil never mentions Horace at all, or indeed the other Augustan authors whose works lasted. But no personal resentment of Vergil got through to the public or to posterity; everyone who mattered must have put the best construction on his reserve.

In short, we have the opposite biographical pattern to the usual one: the childhood seems easier to reconstruct, if only by tentative inferences, while the adulthood is more mysterious. But the imbalanced situation is not merely frustrating; it is also suggestive. A usual font of information about an author in his maturity springs from a settled environment, fixed habits, and long-standing close associates. But from childhood, when he went away to school, Vergil apparently kept moving. There is no evidence that he maintained a country estate, let alone his inherited one, which was usual for an elite Roman who also had a residence in the capital. He never married or had acknowledged children, which was anomalous too, but his fellow poet Horace was also a bachelor (perhaps due to his ambiguous social status as a freedman's son), and this did not prevent him from being comfortably and proudly — and through his verses, visibly — ensconced in both the city and the country. *Why* did Vergil's (literal) groundedness come so early while his later life hovered?

Romans were homey, much given to relaxing and presiding on their real estate and displaying it through hospitality, if not bragging or humble-bragging about their virtuous and tasteful domestic lifestyles. A man of means and position was a man who played the host in his own dining room, spoiled his daughter and married her off to a crony, worried self-importantly about his son's education and future, met with clients, wrote business letters, joshed a favorite slave, and took a lordly interest in productive activities on his estate. From what we read of Vergil's enrichment from literary patronage, he could well have afforded this lifestyle.

He "had" (the verb doesn't convey much) a house adjacent to the gardens of Maecenas, the emperor Augustus' main cultural organizer. Before that, he lived for some years in or near Naples, the choicest resort in Italy, as a member of the kind of posh study circle that Cicero depicts at his villa in Tusculum near Rome. But he spent most of his time "withdrawn" or "retired" in Sicily and Campania (Suetonius, Life 13), the territory whose largest city is Naples, and near the end of his life he embarked on a tour of Greece. If he had an established home of his own, we do not see him in it.

Hence it seems that his lifelong attachment to images of the productive countryside, his characters and stories based there, the importance of the parent-child relationship in his masterpiece the *Aeneid*, and the passion this epic expresses for land as a secure, permanent resting place could have drawn on an especially rich version of the proverbial "bank account" for authors, the earliest years. True, much of this material partakes of his adult literary and political influences and does not necessarily reflect his own first-hand experience, but this does not mean he did not use books selectively and turn a deaf ear to some political demands. The literary resources of the Roman regime, especially after 30 BCE, when it brought under its full control Egyptian Alexandria with its great library, were virtually endless, but Vergil showed quite specific tastes as to his major inspirations. And as I hope to show in Chapter 4, the leeway granted to him under imperial patronage was quite broad; early on, he chose genres, topics, stories, and motifs that were far from the most obviously useful for propagandistic purposes, and when it came to the *Aeneid*, he digressed from the great nationalistic and dynastic theme in many quirky directions.

One of his most affecting creations is the warrior girl Camilla, an opponent of the proto-Roman leader Aeneas. Her father, a deposed king, rescued her as an infant. Pursued through the wilderness by his former subjects and trapped against a stream with a swift and dangerous current, he cannot see how to swim across with the child in his arms, but by a sudden inspiration he ties her to a spear and heaves it to the opposite bank, vowing the child, if she survives, as an attendant to the divine huntress Diana. Both father and daughter escape. In exile in remote mountains, he feeds her straight from a mare's udders and trains and equips her to hunt as soon as she can walk. Camilla may not be an original conception, but if she wasn't, Vergil developed her from obscure antiquarian and folkloric sources that allowed an exotic female character to enter sympathetically into the quintessential Roman story through the narrative vehicle of survival in the wilderness; and he developed her with an insistence on the protective power of fatherhood, even though on the surface this goes against her larger story's grain. Her background is a digression in the portion of the *Aeneid* where warfare is reaching its culminating fury and will annihilate her along the way. It is not unusual to see fatherly care and the countryside come together in the *Aeneid*.

Where did Vergil have more experience of these two things than as a child himself? To explore what these emphases might mean about his life, and whether his literary works more likely reflect a personal reality or a fantasy resistant to one, it seems necessary first to ground him as far as possible in the context of geography, ethnicity, class, and family relations typical of his time.

Vergil came from northern Italy, a region called Cisalpine Gaul, "Gaul on This Side of the Alps." The Gauls were a thorn in Rome's side for centuries; according to Roman annalistic history, a Gallic tribe called the Cenomani took over the city of Mantua (always identified with Vergil) and the region around it a few years before the Gallic invasion of the city of Rome in 390 BCE.

As to Vergil's own ethnicity, his reported swarthiness and tall and stocky body do not exclude many possibilities around the Mediterranean. The linguistic and epigraphic (that is, based on inscriptions) scholarship makes the most of his full name, Publius Vergilius Maro ("Virgilius," from which the English "Virgil" comes, is the dominant Latin spelling, but it is based on an early distortion), and of names ascribed to his parents and maternal grandfather, but no convincing conclusions emerge. He might have been a Gaul, though he depicts Gauls in the *Aeneid* as invading barbarians (8.655–662); he might have been Greek, though books 2 and 3 of the *Aeneid* show the Greeks to be cruel and devious sackers of Troy, inspiring fear and hatred in the Trojan refugees for years afterward; he might have been Ligurian, a race exemplified as devious and cowardly in *Aeneid* 11.699–717.

But there is nothing outlandish about the clan name Vergilius, the "with-name" or cognomen Maro, or, especially, the first name Publius. He might have been ancestrally Latin or Etruscan, meaning a virtual Roman, rustic and not of the city of Rome. But to be a metropolitan Roman meant little in itself: Vergil shows a conventional attitude in depicting a dangerous urban mob that only a respected elder statesman can control (*Aeneid* 1.148–153).

Then again, the poet's fairly recent forebears might have received the *tria nomina,* or traditional three-part name, through a manumission by an Italian or Roman master. Given the prevalence of wars, migrations, and the slave trade and other commercial mobility under Roman hegemony, Vergil's genetics could have derived from anywhere in the accessible reaches of three continents.

Had he not been by all appearances an ancestral, conforming Roman, however, his literary career would have been unthinkable. Italians with home languages other than Latin or other marks of foreign culture stood out, and not to their advantage. Vergil's colleague Horace uses the word "Oscans" (a long-subdued, unpopular ethnic group with a distinct language) as the substance of a punchline (*Satires* 1.5.54). If Vergil projected the right nationality, his mere rustic appearance and slow and almost uneducated-sounding manner of speaking (Suetonius, *Life* 8, 16) could have seemed virtuously simple and old-fashioned (*priscus*) to those inclined to view him favorably.

Cisalpine Gaul did not merge with Roman Italy for administrative purposes until 42 BCE; Vergil, born in 70, would have been around twenty-eight and about to begin his career as an author under the auspices of Octavian and the personal management of Maecenas. For about four decades previously, Cisalpine Gaul had had the status of a province, like a number of Rome's more distant domains. But all the free inhabitants received Roman citizenship in 49, when Vergil was entering adulthood, although individuals born in the province could have had the status of Roman citizens before this. Citizenship typically depended on ancestry, not geography.

What did it feel like to Vergil to be growing up in Italy as at least a technical outsider to Rome? As an issue of future opportunity, location alone probably mattered little; a number of distinguished Roman authors came from outside Italy. And Vergil's homeland was called *Gallia togata*, or "Gaul that wears the toga," the uniform of Roman civic life; Vergil is said to have received his at fifteen (fourteen by modern reckoning; I note these differences where they seem most important), a common age for it. The region was fertile, settled, and prosperous; Vergil completed an expensive education alongside elite Roman youths; former classmates could have become long-term friends and patrons; the future emperor Octavian himself, though he was considerably younger, might have had some of the same teachers as Vergil.

But at that stage of Vergil's childhood and early youth, a native of Cisalpine Gaul might have – with his parents' encouragement – considered himself happily out of the political mainstream and able to adopt a wait-and-see attitude toward Rome. A series of violent convulsions had been going on, which historians collectively call the Roman civil wars; these became particularly frequent and violent during the first century BCE, starting with the Social War of 91 to 87 by which Rome's allies in Italy fought with Rome for equal political rights. Cisalpine Gaul was excluded from the conciliatory settlement, but since greater inclusion meant closer involvement in Rome's turbulence, which was to increase, the settlement might have come to seem like a booby prize. Factions of the Roman governing elite did not even wait for the end of the Social War to begin warring among themselves, and the government was not relatively united again (that is, less prone to dividing violently) until after 77.

The later seventies, the sixties, and the fifties, before Caesar returned from his decade-long conquest of Gaul and reprised full-scale civil wars in 49, brought relative peace to Italy, but in my view Vergil's family may have maintained and passed down to him a sense of relief about their region's relative political detachment. Furthermore, they might have thought they lived in a neighborhood where nothing could happen, near the meandering Mincius River (the modern Mincio), which left rich alluvial soil in the floodplain (Vergil describes the specific place in *Georgics* 3.12–15) – the Italian analogue of the fertile Greek region of Boeotia, reputed to be full of parochial fatheads. How likely is it that when Vergil was still at home, his family even knew about ominous events in Rome or elsewhere until long after they had taken place? Is it significant that when Vergil began to write of war in the *Aeneid,* he depicted cataclysmic battles but set them in a distant, fabulous past, while insisting that Roman violence had yielded peace and order in the here and now?

Because I come from a rural nowhere myself, I know that it is natural to grow tired of naming to uncomprehending listeners the nearest cluster of buildings that has a name, and to start referring instead to the nearest place of note; this gives me confidence that Vergil's hometown was the biographers' Andes, not Mantua, as he himself reports (*Georgics* 3.10–12), and that Andes was a very obscure place indeed. We can take the infrastructure of the ancient world into account in picturing its isolation, given that the best modern candidate to be its descendant, Pietole Vecchia, is only about five miles from Mantua. Until dams were built in the Mincio during the

Middle Ages, it was not navigable, and of course Andes was not on a good main road.

As to the possible long-term influence of origins remote from the center of power and upheaval at the period of the civil wars, comparative experiences that we know more about might be suggestive. Horace, five years younger than Vergil and from Venusia (modern Venosa) in south-central Italy, was pulled into the conflict on the republican side; the rout at Philippi was humiliating in itself (he claims in *Odes* 2.7.9–10 that he abandoned his shield, but he may only be posing in imitation of the shield-losing Greek poet Archilochus) and a sorry influence on some of his writing later, as he strained to publicize a confident, self-respecting yet devoted attitude toward Octavian, the captor of the Roman state. The late-republican poet Catullus was probably ten to fifteen years older than Vergil and from Verona, also in Cisalpine Gaul. His poetry briefly addresses the traditional republican Cicero with sarcasm (Poem 49) and the demagogue Caesar with fearless contempt and obscenity (Poems 29, 57, 93); his one gesture at beginning a political career, a stint on a provincial governor's staff, is crowned with sardonic versified regret that he did not enrich himself with graft in the expected way (Poem 10). Was this a more typical attitude for a geographic outlier during the late years of the republic?

In asking these questions, I question a widely prevailing view of all the major Augustan authors — in addition to Vergil and Horace, they were the love elegists Propertius, Tibullus, and Ovid, the historian Livy, and the polymath Varro — as deeply affected by warfare. In fact, from the Social War to the Battle of Actium in 31 BCE, thirteen of the distinct armed conflicts in which Rome was engaged were between Roman or Italian factions (including rebellious slaves). This list does not even include foreign revolts and other disturbances whose origins and suppression were closely linked to Roman politics, such as Caesar's Gallic wars. For his campaigns, Caesar needed a whole series of appointments as general, whereas the Roman government ordinarily authorized a man to command an army in a province for a year only. He should by no means command an army until it forgot about any leader but him, or bring it back to Rome's home territory, where it could help seize the government—which is what Caesar did, crossing the Rubicon River into Italy in 49 BCE with his armed troops. After Actium, authors as well as the mass of people living under the Roman Empire were probably immensely relieved to be at peace, and not eager to invest their lives in vindicating the old oligarchical republican regime; moreover, selected authors received an outsized share of the new settlement's benefits in the form of official or semi-official patronage. By this account, a generation or more of famous Roman authors, including Vergil, was profoundly affected in childhood and youth by the civil wars and predisposed to favor the Augustan peace.

But something beyond question is that the military conflicts' repercussions eventually reached Vergil's homeland in the form of colonization. Colonization meant that a Roman bureaucracy with an armed force to back it up would confiscate land and distribute it to veterans of a newly victorious Roman army. This happened to Vergil's home district and many others north of the Po River after Octavian's faction defeated Caesar's assassins and their followers in 42. Vergil's remarks at the beginning of *Eclogues* 1 give the impression that his own family farm was taken but returned through Octavian's personal intervention.

MELIBOEUS

You, Tityrus, stretched beneath a beech tree's cover,
Rehearse the forest Muse on your slim reed;
We leave our homeland's boundaries, our sweet fields.

Origins

We flee our homeland. Tityrus, you're slacking in the shade,
Teaching the woods to echo "Lovely Amaryllis."

TITYRUS

It was a god who gave us this leisure, Meliboeus.
He'll always stay a god to me; out of my folds
Young lambs will keep soaking his altar with their blood.
He let my oxen roam, as you see here, and me
Play on my rustic reed pipe whatever I wish.

MELIBOEUS

No grudge here, truly—but I *am* surprised. The havoc
Spreads to all corners of the countryside. Just look: I drive
These goats along beyond my strength—this one I'm scarcely
Dragging, Tityrus: just now, in this thick hazel grove she left
The flock's hope, twins, stillborn on flinty ground.

(1.1–15)

It would be reckless to assume that this passage or any other directly reflects Vergil's or his family's own hardships in the aftermath of war. They probably had trouble over the farm, as Suetonius in this respect is unusually specific. He names three high-level operatives, Asinius Pollio, Alfenus Varus, and Cornelius Gallus, associates of the three-man dictatorship at Rome, the so-called Second Triumvirate. The biographer adds that Vergil dedicated the *Georgics* to Maecenas for coming to his rescue when a dispute with a veteran about the farm nearly got the poet killed (Life 19–20). Vergil himself praises Pollio, Varus, and Gallus in the *Eclogues*. Indeed, in *Eclogues* 9, the subject of rural expulsion is reprised from *Eclogues* 1: two shepherds affirm that "Menalcas" saved a parcel of land "with his songs," but almost died from a "new feud" (7–16);

among "unfinished" poetry of Menalcas is a flattering plea to Varus to spare "Mantua" (26–29), as if Vergil tried to have the entire district exempted and the outcome was still uncertain when the *Eclogues* was published in his early thirties. Perhaps, in political terms, his home did become, and remain, a bad place for the poet.

But against reading too much politics into the passages, the message of the *Eclogues* as a whole is clear: the relationship between the countryside and "singing" is symbiotic but broken; the singers keep quarreling, competing, collaborating, lamenting, languishing, and threatening suicide for the sake of something better than the gorgeous landscape. Every rock, plant, animal, person, and god in it both inspires them and exists for their music, but in such a way as projects the singers beyond them. The singers want love and status, but most of all they want music of unprecedented beauty, which is an infusion from the land but does not find a resting place between these horizons. Vergil's calling was, however painfully, not here. The practical terms of this reality may have been fairly brutal. He could not stay there and be a poet, but if he could not stay there, who would run the farm and its attached businesses? Suetonius reports that both of Vergil's brothers had died (one during childhood), as well as his parents, his father having first gone blind (Life 14). As often with the biographer, the wording is vague, but it seems that by some point in the poet's early adulthood he had lost his entire immediate family.

Vergil's social position by birth and upbringing is harder to construe plausibly than most other dimensions of his origins. There is no dispute that his father was a humble man who made good, but I cannot believe that he was no more than a peasant—a smallholder or tenant who tilled the soil himself—because I cannot square that with his rise. A farmer who had no slaves to do the grunt work could no more compete commercially with his neighbors who did have them than an American freedman could make the most of his small plot if he had no mule: at best, his toil would leave him stuck on the treadmill of subsistence or debt. If dirt farming were the father's origins, he needed a major boost from outside to get away from it. In the passage quoted at the beginning of this chapter, Suetonius shapes sundry reports into a story that Vergil's father impressed his employer, a local court officer, enough to receive the man's daughter in marriage, and that he then bought up land and raised bees. This success speaks to more than the usual modern story of a talented man marrying into his boss's business or using his father-in-law's resources to strike out on his own. In a slave society, in which freedmen who remained attached to their former masters' households were available and trusted to do either their old jobs or new ones and sometimes made their own fortunes with the help of old connections, ordinary wage earners began as out-siders and had more to prove. Granted, a local worthy would nor-mally be looking only among freeborn men for prospective sons-in law, and in an out-of-the-way district the candidates might not be plentiful. Still, Vergil's father must have been clever and diligent to have earned his opportunities and made so much of them.

Beekeeping may simply have been read into the biographical tradition from the *Georgics*, Vergil's second major work, a long poem on farming. But if we take a step back and ask about the *Georgics'* inspiration and design, nothing explains why the author bases the climactic and concluding quarter of this work on this particular branch of agriculture. All four books contain a great deal of non-technical, more literary material, but each centers on a technical topic, and in the first three, this seems reasonable. In the first book, the topic is grain farming (bread and porridge were the basic daily foods of Roman Italy); in the second, it is vines (wine was the ubiquitous Roman drink) and fruit trees, including olive trees (yielding oil for cooking, lighting, and care of the skin); and in the third it is herd animals (the source of the wool used for traditional clothing, including the toga, and of leather, dairy products, and meat) and animals used for work. The fourth book centers on the production of honey, which was by no means a necessity: its main uses were for pastry, sweetened wine, and certain medicines. The prominence of apiculture here is at sharp odds with the mainstream tradition of writing about farming, in which the cultural and economic importance of various branches of the enterprise is proportional to the space given them on paper, and no author appears in danger of becoming mesmerized by the genesis of a niche product.

Granted, bees had mythical prestige, of which Vergil takes account. They are disciplined communitarian workers and protectors of their homes and polities, strictly hierarchical in a way the ancients admired, and were thought to reproduce without the distractions and enervations of sex. In addition, they make the most intensely sweet natural product out of, to the naked eye, nothing. But none of these qualities fully explains Vergil's detailed account of their habits, and how to attract, manipulate, feed, water, and protect them through the seasons and their curious life cycle. Nicander, a poet of Greek Alexandria, wrote a work, most of which is now lost, on beekeeping. But Alexandria produced vast tomes of highly losable encyclopedic material. Why did Vergil seek this scroll out, if he did? And what about the almost suicidal grief of Aristaeus the beekeeper in the *Georgics*? The death of his bees means that his homestead and everything that grows on it might as well go up in flames (4.317–332).

But Aristaeus learns how to expiate the crime for which he is being punished – Orpheus' partner, Eurydice, died as the beekeeper was pursuing her – and obtain a healthy new swarm. Orpheus is doomed, in contrast, to a loss both permanent and excruciating; after his tuneful, showy, and in the end useless descent to Hades to retrieve his beloved, he laments musically until jealous and crazed women tear him to pieces. The beekeeper can live on as happily with his new swarm as if the hapless pair had never existed. It is hard not to see as highly personal this quirky intertwined adaptation of the two stories.

But it would be impetuous to jump to images of the boy Vergil trailing his father on beekeeping rounds or helping with related chores, or forced to stay indoors studying, or painfully exiled to urban schooling, away from the fascinating family business. Still, I find it suggestive that he did know an unusual amount about bees and that the landscape he places them in resembles that of his childhood: well watered, with a mild climate and both meadows and woods. His most obvious mistakes — such as calling the queen a "king" and claiming that bees can spontaneously generate from an animal carcass, rather than just using it as a shelter for breeding — are understandable and must have been universal in the age before microscopy; they would not impinge on beekeeping in practice. In other areas of agriculture, Vergil's accounts are more hit-or-miss, and some are absurd. According to the poems, some people protect newly planted cuttings by "pressing them down from above" with stones and "hugely heavy" tiles or pottery shards (2.350–353). No one who had orchards or watched how young plants grow could have believed that. Also, if Vergil's mysterious "they" really did increase the feed only of stallions during breeding season, while cutting back on the mares' feed, keeping them from water, and overexercising them (3.123–137), then those people must have been content to see fewer mares coming into heat and more miscarrying. These details sound like Vergil's or his literary informants' misogyny speaking in the poem, not animal husbandry as it was practiced. Some advice about bees is brutal, such as tearing off the wings of the "kings" to make swarms settle (4.106–108), but it is not ridiculous.

Boys generally slotted into their father's roles in life. Beekeeping aside, it is easy to read a longing for a lost future on the land into some of Vergil's poetry. He alone among Roman authors singled out the bucolic poet Theocritus as a model. He based his first major work, the *Eclogues,* on his predecessor's *Idylls,* often giving his version a contemporary, Roman cast while maintaining Theocritus' swooning sense of the beauty and musicality of nature. The joy of the countryside is pronounced in *Eclogues* 4, with its images of a new Golden Age of ease and plenty: sheep will even grow their wool pre-dyed and be able to change its color (4.42–45) – perhaps a Theocritean-type hyperbole rendered in comic tones.

The *Georgics,* for its part, shows the productive countryside as a fundamental source of wholesome challenge and rewarding virtue, as well as human sustenance. In book 4, Vergil writes in the first person of having encountered an old man at Tarentum (which is in the south of Italy, so this would have been during the poet's adulthood) whose land was good for neither grain farming nor grazing nor grapes, but who through his ingenuity and hard work produced a number of nutritious and delightful goods, including honey, according to the season (125–146). This kind of description draws on the main literature on farming going back to Hesiod, and also on Alexandrian works celebrating exemplary poor people, like Callimachus' old woman Hecale, who shelters and feeds the hero Theseus. Again, Vergil's sentiments may be in part derivative, but had he wished, he could have derived other sentiments from other sources in the vast emporium of literature. Also to be considered are the *Georgics'* scenes of rural blight and a host of other natural perils, showing that Vergil was not just daydreaming about the country but was aware of how hard life there could be; he took hard living surprisingly seriously, considering how far above it he found himself during his own adulthood.

But what about pottery? Suetonius mentions that some sources attribute this craft to Vergil's father (Life 1), and I am inclined to believe them. Farming snobbery among the Romans was supported by, among many other things, laws limiting the highest class, the senatorial one, from moneymaking through trade. To write about farming was essentially to boast in the tradition of the statesman and windbag Cato the Elder, whose *On Farming* was the Latin foundation of the agricultural didactic genre. (Vergil quotes Cato in *Georgics* 2.412–413.) Pottery manufacturing in Vergil's family background seems plausible because it is a low association for a lofty poet, not one he and his supporters would have talked about, and also because Vergil's biographers had no passage of his poetry to crib this enterprise from. (The workshop Vergil pictures in *Georgics* 4.170–175 and *Aeneid* 8.418–453 is a divine smithy for heroic weaponry, of Homeric pedigree.) The biographical report had to come from somewhere else, and reality is a decent guess.

A father as a bootstrapping man with a mucky manufacturing business would not necessarily have placed Vergil in an abyss below the boys and youths who were to become his social and professional circle. If Cicero's personal letters had not been published posthumously, unreachable to his selection and editing, we would not know that the great orator and proud rural proprietor was also a slumlord. The question of whether a man like Vergil could have kept his father's class and occupation secret — perhaps this in itself was a reason not to make himself at home on his family property in his maturity — can be turned around and aimed outward at others. How can we imagine that even the most refined Roman aristocrats shunned all the sordid opportunities available to them in the far-flung, complex economy of the ancient Mediterranean, and therefore dared to probe and snub people who were functionally their peers? It may be useful to compare the extremely sparse and tactful treatment of West Indian slave labor in Jane Austen's novels, some of whose characters get their considerable wealth from it.

In any event, class and wealth (much unlike, for example, eroticism) do not register in Vergil's work as a source of personal stress; he sees the poor with clarity and sympathy, but he does not appear to identify with them. In the *Aeneid,* all the best people, whether dominant or subordinate, work together in devotion and harmony toward the same communal ends. Wealth, produced as if by magic, changes hands freely: precious objects—even unique heirlooms, divine handicrafts, and magically bred horses—are bestowed without hesitation, and more are always available if needed. (A Classics reading group suggested to me that the refugees from Troy, who purportedly have escaped with their lives, should be pictured dragging large carts around from which they dispense and into which they receive various swag.)

Octavian himself was, notably, not a patrician by descent like his adoptive father, Julius Caesar; his biological father's family were equites (horsemen), a commercial class originally designated to provide their own mounts and equipment for service in the Roman cavalry because they could afford to. Those who have confidently called Vergil's father an eques may have done so mainly because the property requirement for that status was high, and the son was educated for leisure and culture and evidently well accepted among young equites and even patricians. But the class was defined not just by wealth but also by the military and other roles equestrians played in respect to the central government in Rome. This appears to rule Vergil's father out entirely.

However, Suetonius' statement that his father "added signifi-cantly to his small amount of property by buying up woods" points to a substantial country establishment — not of course like the rural estates that famous Romans displayed themselves using for leisure, study, and entertaining away from the city, but a large building with facilities in it or outlying around it to produce most of the food, clothing, and implements for the household and business, and a contingent of slaves to do the work in all its different cate-gories. The pottery factory would have been near or adjacent, the hives and meadows for bees as close as possible. As for separating and spacing out economic and domestic activities, the country nor-mally provided only a less compressed version of the urban heap of functions and functionaries. There was no rationale but gentility for other arrangements, and I doubt that Vergil's childhood home had reached the genteel stage, except as concerns himself and his education.

As for family life, Vergil's biographical tradition gives him two full brothers, one near his age. No sisters are mentioned, but this does not mean that there were none; daughters could remain under the patriarchal radar of historical reporting. The very young Vergil might have played with slave children but would have had to be-have later as if this had never happened.

Married ladies did not usually nurse, bathe, and play with their infants and toddlers; processing wool, spinning, weaving, and su-pervising female slaves in these tasks was considered adequate, in fact exemplary diligence. Many well-to-do women of the late re-public and early empire did even less around the house. One factor might have been that clan, business, and political considerations pushed girls into premature marriage and childbearing; their various stresses would not have conduced to warm and involved motherhood. Cornelia, the mother of the Gracchi, is legendary for the character, intelligence, and devotion from which her sons benefited, but she appears to have had a great many foils. Nor can it be supposed that slave women, who were near the bottom of society, always took up the nurturing slack in gentle and conscientious ways when their owners' backs were turned. Nursemaids are sentimentalized in ancient literature, but I will never forget the sight of a uniformed African maid sitting alone on the grass of a Cape Town park with a posh lapdog: she was hitting it in the face with its leash again and again as it cowered and whimpered.

But I cannot assume that Vergil was neglected or abused. He might have been the darling of all the slaves. His mother might have been nurturing, affectionate, and a mentally stimulating presence, but we do not know anything about her personality or activities as an individual; on the other hand, it was not usual for a son to be communicative about these. We know only that she must have remarried after her first husband's death (or, far less likely, been married to someone before him), as Vergil provided for a half-brother in his will (Suetonius, Life 37): the half-brother is called Valerius Proculus, the nomen and cognomen of a different family, following the male line. But Roman women, who married for the first time not long after puberty and whose husbands tended to be considerably older, commonly outlived them and married again.

On the subject of quasi-maternal care, Vergil's own literary evidence is somewhat disturbing. Here is everything written of the woman who nursed the hero of the *Aeneid:*

> Aeneas' old nurse, you as well, Caieta,
> In dying gave our shores your lasting fame.
> The great West keeps your resting place today

Origins

In glory – if there's glory in the grave.
Loyal Aeneas rendered her due rites,
Heaping a mound up.

(Aeneid 7.1–6)

Caieta is typical of slaves and other underlings who flash into Latin literature at the right moment (here she serves Vergil's interest in geographic nomenclature) with no hint that they have been there all along, or even immediately after a free character is presented as being alone. Still, this is an odd start for a chapter-length book of epic poetry. The old nurse (or an old male tutor like Phoenix in the *Iliad*) could be either a notable character or silent or invisible, but to give only this glint of public commemoration, including a brush-off in terms of the doubtful value of funeral rites (a sentiment absolutely not echoed in the poem when it comes to important men), seems strange. A caretaker of the very young, the first regular provider of food, clothing, touch, cleanliness, and language, should be less liable than most people to come across as an abstraction.

Mothers are even more disquieting presences in the *Aeneid*. Aeneas' mother, Venus, attends to him and her grandson with professed tenderness, but her main means of helping them are deals made far away on Olympus. In 1.407–410, Aeneas protests bitterly at her habit of toying with him and receding from contact. His exasperation on this occasion is certainly credible: as if resisting her very identity as his mother, she has approached him in the form of a lovely virgin huntress. Creusa, Aeneas' wife at Troy and the mother of Iulus, is narratively crucial only in getting out of the way, disappearing as, at her husband's inexplicable command, she follows her family at a distance through a city that is in the throes of invasion and sacking near the end of book 2. The widower will be free to marry the Italian princess Lavinia.

Among the Trojan refugees, all the mature women but one choose to stay behind on Crete in book 5 and to make their homes there (after they run amok owing to divine trickery and burn much of the fleet), while their sons the warriors travel on to Italy: Euryalus' mother is the devoted exception, for whom her son, about to leave on the spy mission in book 9, is anxious to provide. Her later grief over his death is overwhelming, suicidal—and too public: the army's sympathy undermines its will to fight, and prudent leaders order her to be led indoors (473–502).

I divide Roman fathers into two basic kinds, those like Cato the Elder and Horace's father who would not let their children's minders and teachers alone and would clearly have liked to do everything themselves, and the fathers who presided and issued demands at more remote heights. Vergil's father was probably the second, more common kind. We see cold yet looming fathers over and over in the *Aeneid*: Zeus, Anchises, Aeneas, Latinus, Evander, Mezentius, Metabus. Children exist for them mainly in an idealized mental realm or in a remote or even far-fetched future that the children themselves are the sole, and sacrificial, means of creating. Men extravagantly mourn their sons and other men's sons whom they have put in harm's way. The prize for this goes to Mezentius, who only over his son's corpse concedes that fleeing unpunished from his royal crime spree, and thus involving his child in the eventual retribution, was a bad idea (10.849–854).

In real, everyday settings in Roman Italy, fathers were sternly concerned about their sons but dealt with them mainly through delegation. Teachers bore heavy expectations that they would control and perfect their charges but had little power over them except through beatings. The minders of Aeneas' son Iulus (also called Ascanius) are physically closer to the boy, more interactive, and more protective than his father usually is, but they are far from adequate.

For example, Iulus causes cataclysmic trouble when, unattended, he kills a gamekeeper's pet stag (7.477–539).

Though Vergil as a personality is often associated with the hero Aeneas, I think it is at least as useful to look comprehensively at Iulus. He is by far the most complete and interesting child to appear in ancient poetry; he is also a far-fetched literary artifact. He is a "soft-haired" toddler or at least quite a young child at Troy, held in his parents' arms while visited with divine portents of greatness (2.679–698), and then led out, trotting along with little steps beside his father's big ones (2.723–724). Seven years later, when the refugees arrive at Carthage, he is young enough for Dido to dandle his simulacrum in her lap (1.717–718), then the next morning old enough to be given a spirited horse and repeatedly outride others in a hunting party that goes coursing through a valley in pursuit of stags (4.156–157).

In probably less than a year, the Trojans leave for Italy, stopping at Crete, where Iulus' grandfather dies. In the commemorative funeral games, Iulus – though "below the age of puberty" – leads the noble Trojan boys in an elaborate equestrian review, the horses moving in interweaving patterns and the boys miming war. When the women on a nearby beach set fire to the ships, Iulus gallops to the rescue; the men who arrive to deal with the emergency are following his lead (5.544–675).

In Italy shortly afterward, after killing the stag, he takes his first bowshot in war during the subsequent siege, and kills a boasting enemy; but Apollo, though thrilled, takes the guise of one of his minders to warn him off more aggression until he is grown up, and the Trojan leaders follow up in restraining him (9.590–662). But it is *before* this, during the same siege, that he is in a strategy conclave when the young Nisus and Euryalus approach with their proposal to get through the enemy lines with a message for the absent

Aeneas. He graciously authorizes their spy mission and decrees rewards, along with a promise of support for the one boy's devoted mother in case she is bereaved (9.226–280). (For the Romans, the age of majority, before which a young man could not incur financial obligations, was twenty-five.) Before the final battle not much later, he is a novice warrior, receiving protective but stern instructions from his father (12.433–440) — but he is never pictured in close combat, let alone in a battle spree.

Iulus' body and his capacities expand and contract to serve all the narrative's needs, although we might expect this character to be especially clearly conceived and stable: he is, after all, a sort of living providence. Aeneas names and treats him as the reason for his own immense sacrifices. Iulus' prerogatives, to be realized in Italy, stand for all the Trojans' future, and in this sense he is the lynchpin of the world's future salvation. The biographical scenes of Vergil himself as the magical child and prophetic young man needed to keep the empire sound are the sort of fiction to which the author had provided a sturdy framework. But the person behind the legend, to judge by his creation Iulus, felt stretched and compressed from an early age by professedly devoted and beloved people.

A final fact to consider — one I will discuss in full in Chapter 5 — is that Vergil was known in his own time to be, as Suetonius literally put it, "of desire more inclined than usual toward boys" (Life 9). For the poet this does not seem to have been a mere preference but rather his unalterable disposition. And he evidently did not have the traits that made homosexual activity most readily acceptable to the Romans: a catholic erotic assertiveness and voracity, and a general "manliness." Suetonius in fact describes him at his birth as having a "gentle" expression (Life 4); and almost up to its end, the biography attests to Vergil's sensitivity and conflict aversion. He never served in the military, in an era when this was a prestigious rite of passage. His rustic manner as an adult may have helped him avoid suspicion of effeminacy, but he was by no means a tough guy; perhaps he needed the protection of a powerful regime for purposes beyond the fostering of his poetic talent. His poor health — Suetonius catalogues symptoms that we associate with stress — may have started in his boyhood, when it would have carried a certain stigma in itself. Physically weak Roman boys were not supposed to exist; weaklings should have been exposed as babies. We do not see frail boys being coddled year after year, as valetudinarian adults of comfortable means were.

How might Vergil's childhood and early youth have contributed, generally and over the long term, to striking qualities in his poetry? I will speculate in only a couple of directions here; the question is complicated, but I can make a start. First, it seems highly probable that Vergil's backwater origin contributed to his depictions of powerless people. A very small town or a rural district is one with little choice of company, where it is harder to escape acquaintance with the poor and put-upon, especially if one's own family is merely on the way up. On the basis of such a childhood, George Eliot helped open up the Victorian literary scene to a fuller, deeper consideration of humble craftspeople and farmers, put-upon women, small children, and others with no public voice.

Vergil was one of very few ancient authors to turn a serious gaze toward the people it had been usual to view contemptuously, comically, or sentimentally. He more likely knew the representative human beings in his childhood than later, but it was not until his literary maturity that he speculated about the full extent of their dehumanization. He introduces into "war books" of the *Aeneid* (books of evidently later composition) two very obscure people at the moment of their annihilation during the great clashes that will ensure the Trojan refugees a home in Italy. The tragic tenderness of the scenes is the opposite of Homer's tone in depicting a lower-class person — the crude, ugly Thersites, beaten up for his insubordinate complaints, to his own army's amused approval (*Iliad* 2.211–277) — as a throwaway.

Vergil's Menoetes is a convincing person, with poignant memories and an understandable resentment of the use now being made of him, but the verb for his death is one he has to share, so trivial in practical terms is his existence on the battlefield, where he has no status or skill and no one to take any interest in him. Delicately stressing the contrast between the disposable object and the individual, irreplaceable life, the author makes him matter to us.

> Aeneas in one clash slew brave Cethegus,
> Talos and Tanaïs; then sad Onites,
> Peridia's child, a Theban; Turnus killed
> Two brothers from Apollo's Lycia;
> Menoetes too, futile in hating war:
> A poor Arcadian, adept at fishing
> The teeming streams at Lerna — not at serving
> Powerful men. His father sowed hired ground.

$$(12.513-520)$$

The Mincius River near Vergil's childhood home flows from Lake Garda, the largest lake in Italy, and both bodies of water have been abundant fisheries since ancient times, when fish were already a widely depleted resource. The place where it is worthwhile to fish offers no refuge from poverty, raging wars, and indifferent, exploitative generals.

Helenor receives more space, but in a sort of inverse proportion to his valor. A hapless mother has dispatched him as a helpless soldier, and he takes a sensible shortcut out of the world, apparently without bothering to raise his weapon.

> When the defenders backed away to huddle
> In a safe place, their weight collapsed the tower,
> And the sky echoed with the sudden crash.
> Dying, they fell, impaled on their own spears
> And the hard splinters — then the huge mass followed.
> Only two crawled out, Lycus and Helenor.
> This last, a youth sired by a Lydian king
> On the slave Licymnia, was born in secret
> And sent by her to Troy, though banned from war.
> His arms were light: an unheroic shield
> With no device, a bare sword. Latin columns
> Flanked him now. He saw Turnus' men in thousands,
> And as a wild thing ringed in tight by hunters
> Lashes against their spears and leaps on purpose
> To perish on their weapons, so the young man
> Rushed in to die among his enemies,
> Making for where he saw the spears were densest.

(9.539–555)

But I think that Vergil's negativity about other people goes beyond frustration rooted in early family relationships and sadness about the suffering of the poor. When I combine a reading of Roman social history with a reading of his poetry, I am convinced that from childhood on, he found his pleasure and satisfaction less in fellow human beings than elsewhere. This would have been a profoundly un-Roman attitude in the greatest Roman poet, but often a writer speaks impressively to his own society by a kind of subversion.

With high confidence, I would posit that from his earliest years Vergil loved the relative quiet and openness of the country, as well as its various natural beauties. Many other Romans felt basically the same way, and if they could afford it set up urban pleasure grounds to mimic the countryside's meadows, groves, and bodies of water. But young writers-to-be may go deeper and, like Tolstoy or J. M. Coetzee, experience a rural place almost as a drug.

Here is a passage of the *Aeneid* that suggests this kind of sensation.

> Now monstrous visions haunted that poor woman.
> Frenzied, she ran amok all through the city,
> Like a top flitting under coiling whip blows;
> Boys in intent play, in an empty courtyard,
> Send it in spacious circles. At the lash,
> It rushes on its curving course. The young group
> Watches in wonder as the blows inspire
> The flying boxwood. No less fiercely driven,
> Amata ran straight through the haughty city.

> (7.376–384)

The simile is for the Latin king Latinus' wife, Amata, possessed by a Fury as she responds to the Trojan refugees' challenge to her daughter's betrothal. The girl was to wed a neighboring prince, an object of some erotic interest for the older woman herself. As usual, Vergil is working from a dense literary background, which is described in line-by-line commentaries on his work, and there may be more precedents here than have survived for scholars to track down. The top had previously been a metaphor for physical and emotional turmoil. But as usual for Vergil, especially where place is concerned, the images are not simply borrowed. Instead of his predecessors' mechanical perception and superficial cleverness in comparison, Vergil develops an impressive atmosphere that gives the reader a sense of real experience. Lucretius set useful examples for Vergil as to resonant phrasing and memorable imagery, but when Lucretius comes up with one telling phrase, such as "to the shores of light" (for entities coming into existence), he uses it again and again; Vergil pickily, marvelously varies every expression. The adult relentlessly composing is as if joined to the child blissfully staring at a world that is never the same from moment to moment but reliably entrancing.

Amata's launch on her heedless frenzy, which will destroy her household along with so much else (including her life: she eventually hangs herself), is compared to an object in a scene of domestic peace and shared diversion. If this is indeed a country house like that of Vergil's childhood, a realistic reason for there being one top and several boys is that the playmates of the small heir are the young *vernae*, home-born slaves. But all the boys are equally enraptured at the top's motion, all equally untroubled by the practicalities of the house or by frustrations and alienations looming in later years. Outside, in a distant city, in the legendary past, a woman is charging around on grim adult business. That only makes the scene within the frame more enchanting.

Among other such scenes is this one:

Meanwhile, great waves of worries tossed the hero,
The son of Troy, at everything he saw.
His thoughts were darting one way, then another,
At every side of his perplexity,
Like shivering light reflected from the water

In bronze urns, from the sun or shining moon;
Flittering all around, then shooting upward
To strike the panels of the lofty ceiling.

(8.18–25)

Here again, within the very turbulent, very adult concerns is a zone of peace, and it is even more peaceful than the scene with the playing boys. Bronze urns suggest the work of the household, but no one is doing it at the moment; no people appear in the scene. Like many of Vergil's images of space, this one is strikingly vertical, as if a child with plenty of time on his hands is looking upward in delight.

In general, it is remarkable how much feeling, drama, and sheer poetic ingenuity Vergil concentrates not on *people's* but on *scenery's* changes, making the land the enthralling lead actor, the main evolving personality. Sometimes in the *Georgics,* and often in the *Aeneid,* the world is viewed from incredibly steep angles and great distances. Across immense vistas in the epic, birds migrate or flee predators. Gods ascend or descend dizzily. Animals rush down mountains to fight. Fires, floods, landslides sweep through in their destruction. The workings of a volcano are shown from its subterranean roots (a defeated monster is pinned under it) clear up into the atmosphere full of flaming and smoky debris, terrorizing the travelers who spend the night in the vicinity (3.570–587). Vast chasms and swamps bisect the underworld in book 6. A natural disaster can rearrange the world, as at the Straits of Messina:

They say some cataclysm split these places.
(Time holds within it such tremendous changes.)
It was a single place once, but the waves
Burst through the middle, splitting Italy

From Sicily, to sever farms and cities
By the new shores and narrow, sweeping tides.
Scylla lurks on the right, vicious Charybdis
On the left; its vortex sucks down vast cascades
Sheer to the bottom three times every day
And spouts them back to strike the stars with froth.

(3.414–423)

The thrumming counterpoint to this far-reaching violence is the close-range cinema of rustling leaves, flowers, grass, waves, river water, gentle wildlife and livestock, and a thousand other such features of the lovely and living earth. Few things are seen at the usual angle, however, and some are seen at an angle not then possible for human beings: birds in lofty flight, for example, are typically seen from above or from the side, so that their emotion or their own view earthward is communicated.

One frequent criticism of Vergil's poetry is just: his people are relatively stilted. The speakers in the *Eclogues* are for the most part poseurs, Alexandrian-inspired effetes dressed as herdsmen for a pantomime about life in the mountains. The *Georgics* has little space for humans (and one of them, the beekeeper Aristaeus, lives only for his bees, a circular characterization convenient in a work on agriculture). Characters in the *Aeneid* tend to be wooden, without plausible inner lives. Too many of their motivations are literally external, depending on commands or meddling from the gods.

In the case of a poet like Vergil, it is unsatisfying to blame this on the underdeveloped state of literary characterization in his time. With effort, he could develop anything he felt like: his language, his meter, obscure genres, clunky images, shopworn rhetoric. I am convinced that his characters tend to fall short in differentiation and believable thoughts and feelings because he did not like other people much or find their minds reliably interesting compared with his own. The land, in contrast, was endlessly fascinating to him.

He makes gestures of personal withdrawal, approach, and control related to the land and literature, as if these are his real society. At the end of the *Eclogues*, he shows himself retreating with his goats from the pleasant shade of shared pastoral song because shade "hurts" the crops. (At the time he was beginning or about to begin the *Georgics*, on farming.) At the start of the *Georgics'* third book, in another of his few ventures into an "I," he dreams of fluttering above the "soil." Then, appearing to be carried away by the confidence that thoughts of the land bring him, he proposes returning to Mantua to host celebrations for Octavian, and it is actually "I, a victor for him," who will be dressed in royal Tyrian purple, as the driver leading a hundred four-horse chariots beside the stream of the Mincius (8–18); he appropriates Octavian's traditional military Triumph but only in this special place. The festivities will include a theatrical performance (24–25); Suetonius reports that the *Eclogues* was successful enough to be staged many times with musical accompaniment (Life 25). The poetry has represented the land, and now the land can represent the poetry, a typically bold Vergilian reversal.

By the time he wrote the *Aeneid*, Vergil had fully internalized both the actual land as he knew it, the land in literature as it stood, and the land in its political and emotional dynamics, and he let it unwind in a new kind of beauty. This motion helped make his work dreamlike and full of an otherworldly power. He could finesse the realities as someone who rode above them, like his gods and his birds, or inside them, like the infernal beings; and his power was greater than Orpheus', because his words would last.

CHAPTER TWO

Three Kinds of Literary Education

Suetonius reports that Vergil's speech as a young man was extremely slow and sounded almost uneducated (Life 16). It startles me to read this about someone who would become a great Roman author, for the Romans prized oral command of language. Vergil is also supposed to have been a "rustic-looking," reticent, and retiring man (Life 8, 11), and as such would have stood out in the elite and cosmopolitan circles where he eventually found himself. The biographical fallacy may have done some work here, drawing on poetic subject matter with so much in it of the country-side, and on fictional characters with isolating vocations (herding, beekeeping), and applying this "evidence" directly to the author. Nevertheless, I do not want to treat this description of Vergil lightly, if only because it is consistent with other things reported about him.

Criticisms of Vergil's work by his contemporaries hold special interest, especially when backed up by modern study of his literary Latin. Suetonius (Life 43) cites the parodist Numitorius, who nastily accuses Vergil of questionable Latin, "the way they talk out in Aegon's country," but this is not an empty sneer: *cuium* really is a striking variation on *cuius* (whose). (Aegon is the owner of a herd of cows who has gone off to compete in the Olympics in Theocritus' *Idylls* 4, so he could be a byword for an overambitious yokel.) And even as a reverent, longtime lover of Vergil, I cannot protest loudly against the other lampoon by Numitorius that Suetonius quotes ("Tityrus, if you have a warm toga, then why the beech cover?"), of the first line of the *Eclogues*, where the metaphor for shade is literally the "covering of a beech tree" that Tityrus is lying under: it does sound in Vergil as if the herdsman is huddled under a bark or leaf blanket, not the large wool toga that shielded a respectable Roman from the elements. Vergil in modern languages arrives as a reverent gift from translators like myself, buffed into a seemly sheen so as never to seem uncouth or weird. But as in the case of all revolutionary poetics, its expressions *became* exemplars of refined taste and impeccable usage; they did not start out that way. The author's popularity changed the standards.

Another odd hint about Vergil's development comes from a quite late biographical source, the fifth-century CE commentator and antiquarian Macrobius, who mentions that Vergil studied Greek (the language? the literature?) with the scholar Parthenius (*Saturnalia* 5.17.18), whom he would have known at the rough equivalent of a college or even graduate school level of his own scholarship. Cultivated Romans no doubt exaggerated when they conveyed that things Greek were second nature to them, but even so, how much tutoring would Vergil have needed after so many years in a dual-language educational system? Perhaps he merely needed orientation in Theocritus' unusual Doric Greek in the *Idylls*, which were the template for the *Eclogues*. In any case, *Eclogues* 8.58 contains a rookie mistake: Vergil apparently could not distinguish in Greek between "changed to the contrary" (in the sense of "upside down" or "against nature") and "in the [middle of] the sea."

Add to this the modern consensus that none of the juvenilia ascribed to Vergil (for more on which see the next chapter) would make a literary agent sit bolt upright; add also the consistent and plausible testimony that he worked at an extremely slow rate and was a morose, unconfident perfectionist literally until his death, and the outline forms of a man who, even as he reinvented literature, never stopped struggling.

How, then, can we start to picture Vergil's education in relation to his poetic calling, thinking back to — at the latest — the stage at which he made an impression by lampooning a teacher in verse as a living piece of heavy siege artillery (Suetonius, Life 17)?

In his time and place, things could not have been easy for the poetically gifted, no matter how obvious the gift. Educational opportunities for all boys depended on decisions that caused trouble and anxiety for far better resourced and more sophisticated parents than Vergil's; for one thing, teaching as a profession did not tend to attract Romans who had a choice, so educating a child might well entail putting him in foreigners' hands at important stages to learn the gods knew what — perhaps even lewd dancing.

Families, possibly including Vergil's, who could afford it employed tutors at home for the rudiments or beyond; but accessing, selecting, and monitoring these functionaries was easier for urban, educated, and well-connected parents. A comic passage from the Roman novelist Petronius (who wrote in the mid-first century CE) depicts a parvenu freedman telling how he is schooling either two sons through one tutor or one son through two — it is hard to be sure, so clumsy is the account. In one swift progress report, the speaker mashes up rudimentary arithmetic, Greek literature, Latin literature, the prospect of legal study from newly acquired books, and the possibility — if the boy does not prove studious — of having him trained to be a barber, an auctioneer, or at least a forensic advocate; but the speaker *starts* with the assurance that the boy will study with the professional rhetoric teacher to whom he is addressing this disquisition (*Satyricon* 46). The freedman's oafish language indicates the depth of the muddle he is in: the key for a boy to join the elite was in fact rhetoric, obsessively imbibed. How will a father like this keep him at it?

Petronius' send-up suggests how absurd Horace's freedman father, officiously accompanying his son from one elite teacher to another but insisting that he would have been content to see the boy turn out to be an auctioneer or a revenue agent (*Satires* 1.6.81–87), might have appeared to the Roman aristocracy. Would Vergil's father, no freedman but probably not erudite or suave, have been more or less useful for being involved or not involved in his son's education? And how long did it take to unite in one person a recognition of the boy's particular talents and interest with skill in developing them?

If the young Vergil never had a tutor, then he depended wholly on schools distant from his home. Schools were not plentiful during the late republican period, and some district hubs did not have any, or not good ones. Besides the usual Roman paranoia about what children were doing when out of sight in places where foreigners presided, doubts arose about the quality of instruction in the unregulated system, and about the quality of classmates in times of increased social mobility. Horace's schooling could have started, or maybe did start, in rustic obscurity alongside "the big sons of big centurions," the bruiser lowest class of Roman officialdom (*Satires* 1.6.72–75). Horace's father did not want him in such a school and invested daringly in bringing him to Rome to study under the second most prestigious instructors in the world; the most prestigious were the philosophers and rhetoricians at Athens, to whom the young man was dispatched in due course.

There must have been no school, or none deemed suitable, at Mantua, or Vergil would not have gone as a child to Cremona, a distance of more than forty miles. The move probably required not only a small household to be set up for him there but also an entourage such as the one Horace describes taking him to classes in Rome. Horace's father led his son's entourage, a move depicted as so unusual — in this case it meant a freedman's reverting to duties of a slave in order to help on the spot as his son rose steeply in the world — that I doubt Vergil had his father with him in Cremona. Against this argument, Poem 8 of the "Slight Poems" section of the *Appendix Vergiliana* does indicate that the father was with him in that city; but the poem appears to be garbled and historically suspect. And wouldn't Suetonius' sources, and Suetonius himself, have noted the odd circumstance of the father's presence?

After Vergil's assumption of the toga of manhood at fifteen, he had further schooling in Milan, a regional hub, but did not stay long before continuing to Rome. He then went for philosophical inculcation to Naples, rather than Athens. Perhaps his family could not afford to send him to Greece, or the journey and sojourn seemed too risky during the period in question. The far-flung civil war that Julius Caesar waged with the senatorial faction lasted from 49 until 45 BCE, at which point Vergil was in his mid-twenties. In any event, his desire to see Greece resulted much later in a dicey and possibly rebellious journey, and after returning abruptly from Athens with his chief patron the emperor, he died in an Italian port in 19 BCE.

As to the basics of Vergil's training, we know a fair amount of context. The best sources on elite Roman education are Cicero and Quintilian. Cicero was born in 106 BCE, and was a man of sublimely public-spirited cultivation, at least according to himself. But preparation to take part in governance may have held much less interest for a youth of Vergil's generation after Sulla had shown the fragility of the republic in a way no one could mistake, setting Julius Caesar the example of a march on Rome and a military dictatorship. Exemplifying someone whose life spanned the change, Cicero had learned the Twelve Tables, the basic Roman law, as a boy, and as an adult he lamented that this part of the curriculum had fallen away (*On the Laws* 2.59). He is a sort of patron saint of attorneys, but in everything he did he was a politician. Having gotten into trouble in Rome, he found himself relegated to his rural villa, issuing treatises on rhetoric, philosophy, morals, divination, and other topics, but their main purpose was evidently to advertise what a civilized statesman he was. His study of poetry resulted in a notorious verse memoir, *On His [Own] Consulship*. It was only over public rhetoric that he really sweated, and only there did he produce original masterpieces.

Vergil's retiring personality and his serious interest in poetry might seem the obvious reasons he chose not to enter the profession of forensic advocacy for which he had prepared. Suetonius says he conducted a single case before quitting — and here the slow and uneducated manner of his speaking is explicitly connected to the dead end in his legal career (Life 15–16). Perhaps he failed on purpose in order to have more control over his time, a plain concern later in his life. But what happened in the end to Cicero himself, the greatest orator Italy had ever produced, would have given Vergil reason enough never to regret the end of a career that had placed him personally in the civic spotlight. Cicero was assassinated by thugs of Mark Antony, and his head and hands were cut off and displayed on the Rostra (speaker's platform) at Rome from which he had proclaimed to enthralled crowds his defiance of Antony's lawless power grabs (Appian, *The Civil Wars* 4.appendix). The assassination took place in 43 BCE; four or five years later Vergil released his first major work, the *Eclogues,* which was mainly about herdsmen in remote pasturelands but also glorified the first emperor and members of his circle.

Quintilian (who was born around 35 CE), as a "professor of oratory" and the head of a public school, was an actual professional teacher. He was a sometime statesman and legal advocate too, but by this era, when the empire was well established, matters of public controversy had long lain outside a prudent man's expressed concerns. Quintilian peddled a system of guidance and discipline in every detail, down to the stencils that accustomed pupils to draw letters (*Training in Oratory* 1.1.27). The literature he prescribes is wide-ranging and high in quality; of course he includes Homer and Vergil. But the pinnacle at which all this training aimed was panegyric of the reigning emperor; a milestone was Pliny the Younger's panegyric of Trajan in 100 CE. The elite's tastes and mindset had congealed so solidly that schooling in oratory remained fully enforceable even when it had no more useful or more dignified goal than the ceremonial flattery of an autocrat.

In Vergil's youth, the demand for rhetorical excellence had not yet been mitigated by Quintilian's interest in how boys could learn most naturally and pleasantly. The swashbuckling corporal punishment he would frown on was still undisputed, and a number of important Latin titles on Quintilian's reading list did not exist yet. (Latin literature has no indigenous genres – if we do not count some obscure parts of the folk culture – except satire, and so had to borrow hugely and, early on, pretty awkwardly from Greek.) The snorting-warhorse patriotism and rigid moralism typical of the archaic Latin authors left sophisticated late republican students cold.

The brutal republican classroom discipline and the brutalist republican curriculum went together. Horace and Vergil may both register this connection satirically. The former remembers a teacher as a "flogger" (*Epistles* 2.1.70–71) – the image seems to be of gashes opened across the victim's back. The earliest verses ascribed to Vergil (Suetonius, Life 17) are a schoolboy's gloating epitaph, probably joking that a teacher was at last stoned to death with the heavy artillery he had deployed against his charges: "Under this massive heap of stones, the Catapult is interned. / Traveler, you can now go on your way safely either by day or night." The verses bring to mind the monster Cacus (Bad Guy), the bandit of *Aeneid* 8.190–267, whom Hercules throttled to death after ripping open his cave: the mound of ruins is pointed out to the Trojan visitors as a memorial to the quashing of bestial evil and the establishment of civilized safety in Pallantium, the proto-Rome.

That the young Vergil may have satirized a teacher, as his fellow poet Horace did as an adult, suggests one reason his schooling did not sink him. Dislike of teachers can increase solidarity among students otherwise prone to fight among themselves. Vergil probably also gained from school the habit of keeping his head down, interacting inoffensively with bad literature, and convincing those more powerful than himself of his goodwill and best efforts when his thoughts and ambitions were elsewhere, or even tinged with contempt for those around him. No one, evidently, had a smoother surface in a philosophical and literary coterie than Vergil did; though his rage is palpable in his work, he got through a life of celebrity without acquiring important enemies. His social address would also license the withdrawal and private time he needed to become the first modern author: obsessive and haunted in his aesthetics, idiosyncratic and uncompromising in his joy and despair, rising above public performance to a new kind of permanence — a world to himself.

Some details can illustrate what Vergil had to get through and beyond, and may help explain his personal emotional suppression and aesthetic wildness as an adult. The old Latin literature, along with classic Greek works, formed the basis for an education that started around the age of seven and in many cases extended well into adulthood. (As noted, the Roman age of majority, at which a man could incur his own financial obligations, was twenty-five, and this suited the notion that wobbly youth needed stable tutelage.) The primary teacher (*litterator*, or, in Greek, *grammatistes*) and the secondary one (*grammaticus*) both had titles meaning "man of letters," and at the tertiary level presided the rhetorician, the "man of speaking."

Such titles signal the intense focus on language, with which little more than arithmetic competed at the first stage, and little more than literary trivia in the second. Whereas our system puts a great deal of effort into making a child reflexively numerate, using reams of arithmetic problems, a standard Roman drill used challenging letter combinations to perfect pronunciation. At least at this early stage of language training, the consequences for failure were grave; and since many of the demands were not age-appropriate, grave consequences abounded. The first-century CE poet Martial satirizes the local schoolteacher as a noise nuisance because of his bellowings and beatings (*Epigrams* 9.68).

As the training progressed, what modern educators treat as separate academic subjects—history, geography, and so on—figured mainly as the content of literature. Literature in turn underpinned oratory, but loose or inspirational teaching techniques ("Describe how this poem makes you feel") were unthinkable. Teachers relied heavily on reading aloud and recitation, which yielded later on to oratorial exercises in which striking cleverness had somehow to observe countless shallow proprieties, as in gesturing, for example.

Among the Roman elite, who did not play on sports teams, seek prizes at the Olympics and other international games, subject themselves to any modern type of meritocratic bureaucracy, or even hold what we would call free and fair elections, competition was disproportionately packed into oratory. This led to a special verbal gamesmanship that spilled out of the classroom to be practiced by adults: declamation. Declamation employed redramatized episodes from history and literature and far-fetched hypothetical legal cases. In book 11 of the *Aeneid,* the debate between Drances and Turnus in the Latin kingdom's assembly concerning war and peace (343–444) is a virtuoso *controversia,* or pair of dueling declamatory speeches. Vergil works in some telling cracks against the accomplished speaker Drances, thereby effecting a rhetorically skillful condemnation of rhetorical skill, a trick popular since Plato.

But we do not know whether Vergil ever wished to be a skilled orator himself. We have no idea what happened the single time he pled a case in court (if he actually did), or whether he left the profession voluntarily or in the certainty that he would never have another client. It is evident only that he had oratory's number as a highly artificial mode of communication waning in attractiveness and relevance.

Among the evidence is this poem in the *Appendix Vergiliana* ("Slight Poems" 5), notable for its sweetness and gentleness, and considered one of the most likely in the collection to be Vergil's own.

> Get out of here, you rhetoricians' empties,
> Overblown words, not Attic, more like screeching:
> And you, Seliuses, Tarquitiuses, Varro,
> A polity of fathead, head-stuffed nerds;
> Out of here, hollow gong that rings in youth's ears.
> And you, Sextus Sabinus, love of loves,
> Farewell, and farewell now, you gorgeous boys.
> We raise the sails, set off to happy harbors,

Seeking the learned teachings of great Siro;
We'll free our life of every sort of care.
Get out, you Muses too, yes, even you now,
Sweet Muses (since I must confess the truth:
You *were* sweet). Well, consider you're invited
To my pages — but come modestly, and seldom.

Here Vergil or his plausible persona dismisses his oratorical training, and along with it the whole workshop of bookish pedantry.
What he does *not* dismiss are the friendships he enjoyed in school;
the erotically exuberant warmth he expresses toward those he
leaves behind signals that he will happily spend time with similar
people where he is going. And he is moving toward two fields of
endeavor that, closely paired in this poem, might have been twin
or even overlapping passions: philosophy — Siro was an Epicurean
teacher; Vergil also studied with one called Philodemus — and literature. These two fields, and the new friends whom he could cultivate, must have made for a propitious few years of his life, after
which he emerged as a protégé of the Roman emperor with a brilliant first major publication, the *Eclogues*.

But in the poem, the speaker powerfully favors literature. He
gives it the final four lines, and contradicts his coy dismissal of the
Muses: they are too enticing to send away for good. In warning
them not to visit pushily or frequently, he makes a show of mod-
erating his hopes. But the reader knows from the charm of the
poem that the Muses and the writer will get on like old friends.

Such sentiments seem to jell at the end of the *Georgics*, in the
coda (or "seal") where the strong "I" of the poet reemerges after
the plans at the start of book 3 to celebrate Octavian in person in
Vergil's hometown. Now Vergil writes that "sweet Naples" has
"nourished" him as he "throve in pursuits belonging to inglorious

leisure," while Octavian thunderously triumphed in the East. The poem ends with Vergil admitting that he was "bold in/with youth" as he wrote pastoral verse, and his last line is a quotation of the *Eclogues*' first one. By this point in his career, I cannot discern through his writing that he went south to do anything but write, let alone that he was ever a philosophical disciple.

I would also not put much stock in Suetonius' assertion that Vergil studied medicine and mathematics (Life 15), though he might have shown an interest in them. The natural sciences had been under the philosophical heading ever since pre-Classical times in the Greek-speaking world. Some medical writers, for example, belonged to the philosophical school of the Skeptics. Epicureanism contained a literal universe of natural-science assertions and interwove them with teachings about ethics and metaphysics. But when it came to members of the Roman elite with a philosophical bent, the last thing technical topics would likely do was foster a professional calling. I think we can just forget about Vergil as an aspiring doctor or mathematician.

We are also free to doubt how seriously the Romans took philosophy itself, and Vergil is a case in point. He certainly did not remain an exclusive, doctrinaire Epicurean, if he had ever been one, but used philosophy in flexible literary modes, a familiar habit even among Roman authors who professed allegiance to one school or another. In both the *Eclogues* (6.31–34) and the *Aeneid* (6.724–727), words that appear to be more germane to Stoicism than Epicureanism tell of matter's origins, but immediately after in the *Aeneid* the Pythagorean doctrine of reincarnation surfaces, presumably because that works best in the narrative there. Vergil shows in the underworld a parade of Roman heroes, souls who will be purified and then sent back to the mortal world and embodied in future history. Epicureanism would not work here at all; it is a materialist philosophy, according to which human beings have only the body, and no soul to experience preexistence or an afterlife. Epicureanism does not work well in the *Aeneid* overall: the epic's gods are passionately partisan and powerfully involved in history, whereas Epicurus maintained that the gods were distant and indifferent. Nor does a purist Epicureanism work for the *Eclogues* and the *Georgics*, both of which profess a deep reverence for poetic achievement; Epicurus had been no friend of the arts and culture. Moreover, the *Georgics* endorses every effort and every existential anxiety around farming: Epicurean ethics are fundamentally about the peace people can achieve when they stop striving to get ahead. How did Vergil, a literary striver in his bones, fall in with this philosophy in the first place?

What might provide the best answer is his tendency to echo the Roman Epicurean poet Lucretius. These are mainly literary echoes, of phrasing and scenery and drama, and almost never does a specific doctrinal message survive the transition to the later author. In one instance where an Epicurean idea is plainly audible, it comes from Dido's sarcastic and hysterical mouth, and it is false: the gods in the *Aeneid*'s world are *not* indifferent to the fate of human beings, as she claims (4.376–380).

Lucretius himself notoriously opens his poem *On the Nature of the Universe* with a celebration of the goddess Venus, shown as very much present on earth in the springtime and making all life possible through erotic desire — a state that Epicurus had feared and condemned as the enemy of calm and inner peace. Epicurus would have disapproved of a long, elaborate poem in itself as a frivolous and wearing use of mental energy. But in the ancient world, philosophy always loses, and literature always wins.

Moreover, the cultural weakness of philosophy, as a *discipline*, seems broader than this. The Romans reduced the pursuit to little more than a way to put the finishing touches on a gentleman's education. These touches were in large part social, as conversation played very important roles in ancient philosophy. Cicero adopted the verbal exchange (real or imagined) as a literary mode for Roman use; he included in his dialogues respected and likable people from his political and social and cultural milieus, and concentrated on making them and himself look good. Moral aspiration, spiritual enlightenment, and an expansion of the boundaries of thought were hardly the points of the exercise.

Vergil may have gone to Naples mainly to be with congenial people, and in the confidence of finding them in philosophical circles — that is, if he did not know any of them from before. He may have drawn encouragement from Epicureanism's emphasis on friendship pursued in a pleasant withdrawn place, exemplified by Epicurus' own garden. For a man with Vergil's sexual disposition who was nearing marriageable age and was within the age for having "female friends" or mistresses, a philosophical retreat must have offered an especially safe environment. The exclusion of women from the philosophical domain (though not sanctioned by Epicurus himself, whose own gatherings were strikingly egalitarian) was almost complete, whereas Roman women attended dinner parties, festivals, sporting events, and other public entertainments, frequented urban amenities, traveled to and relaxed at country estates and seaside resorts — in short, they were present for most of the leisure activities men took part in, and even respectable women expected attentions specific to their sex. This must have irritated a man at the stage of life when his libido was most powerful if that libido excluded women, so naturally Vergil preferred all-male social settings.

But the expression of his libido could not have been strikingly aggressive. Naples was where Vergil reportedly acquired the nickname Parthenias, literally, "Virginal." The reason was probably not just that his Greek tutor was named Parthenius or that his own name is not far from the Latin for a young, sexually inexperienced girl, *virgo*. The pun likely indicated that he had no mistress and did not frequent brothels. But if he was dividing most of his time between his solitary literary activities and his philosophical discussions, his friends may have classed him as a lofty soul rather than a freak or a killjoy. His habit of withdrawing, and the inclination of his friends to want more of him than they could get, might have solidified in these years as a way to avoid heterosexual pressures and embarrassments as well as to reserve more time for his work.

And, again, no pressure or embarrassment would have come from his philosophical "studies." At the Bay of Naples, many wealthy Romans had villas, gardens, and pleasure boats to enjoy. If philosophy was another occupation, it was not disciplined or morally binding. This is not how adult Romans treated the Greek philosophical experts they had on their payrolls. Vergil and his companions would have had a pleasant time communing with one another and their sages and hearing a version of Epicureanism that suited them.

The crowning piece of evidence for what Vergil's Neapolitan sojourn would have been like is the approximately eighteen hundred papyrus scrolls excavated from the town of Herculaneum, which was engulfed in volcanic ash and lava during the eruption of Mount Vesuvius, near Naples, in 79 CE. Most of the scrolls are associated with none else but the Epicurean philosopher Philodemus, and they were found in a luxurious villa. Epicurus, the advocate of plain living, would not have rejoiced to know that such a place enshrined books written under his aegis. But for the villa's owner, the historical substance of Epicureanism was no barrier to his lifestyle. Maybe to Vergil, as to Cicero's friend Atticus, adherence to this philosophy meant little more than lengthy and posh seclusion, into which only interesting and congenial people could penetrate: conditions ideal for literary pursuits.

The mid-first-century BCE literary circle of the Neoterics (a Greek-derived word used deprecatingly of them and meaning "recent") shows an attitude of exploratory cliquishness that must have appealed to Vergil, though he came to Rome too late to belong to the circle. These men embraced the poetry of the Greek city Alexandria near the outlet of the Nile. A couple of centuries earlier, the dynasty of the Ptolemies, inheritors of Alexander the Great's conquered Egypt, had drawn authors from all over the Greek world and established a massive library that fed their work and employed some of them. The effective spokesman for their ethos was the poet Callimachus, who flaunts his exquisite refinement in contrast to the dullness and bombast of epic. There lived in Alexandria, however, a prominent epic poet, Apollonius of Rhodes, whose tale of the *Argo*'s mythical voyage was useful to Vergil for the *Aeneid*. But across genres and forms, the Alexandrians were to a large degree united in their originality, their learning, and their esotericism. Nicander's works include a poem on venomous animals (which is extant) and one on beekeeping (lost except for fragments), which may have been an important source for Vergil's *Georgics*.

The Alexandrian output was uninspiring as a rule, but it did communicate one enthralling fact: for these authors, the entirety of Greek literature was an open warehouse full of costumes to try on, cut up, and refit at will. Roman and Greek literature in the Roman classroom functioned as a straitjacket, with rigid stays of patriotism, moralism, and superficial cleverness to restrict the young orator. The Alexandrians made literary-minded Romans realize they could do just about anything: plunder existing genres, forms, and topics and reshape them as they wished; explore inside alien heads without the stagy, public-oriented judgment typical of Classical Greek and early Roman literature. Catullus has an Alexandrian-style epyllion (little epic), Poem 64, with a credible portrait of a young, seduced girl's erotic abandonment; the *Ciris,* attributed to Vergil, is a competent epyllion with a lovesick, desperate girl as its heroine. Vergil chose as a model for his first major work, the *Eclogues,* the bucolic *Idylls* of the Alexandrian poet Theocritus, who lacked previous Roman champions but proved a worthy developer of this one's musical gifts and topical interests. The second poem of the *Idylls* yields the "Sorceress" section of *Eclogues* 8, perhaps the most closely copied from a Greek model of all Vergil's passages; it is the lament of a young enchantress for her absconding seducer and a chilling staging of her spells and rites to draw him back.

But today's academy may have exaggerated the influence of the Alexandrians and other Hellenistic authors on the Neoterics. Greek lyric poets of the Archaic period were clearly major models, as they would be to Horace later; for example, Catullus translates a poem by Sappho quite closely and quite beautifully (Poem 51). He also echoes Homer and Euripides, who had hoary Roman translators. True, there were authors in mid-century Rome whom Cicero could sneer at as "chanters of Euphorion" (*Tusculan Disputations* 3.45). (Euphorion was a court poet and librarian in Syria, not Alexandria, but he was the classic Alexandrian type: obscure, precious, and allusive.) Yet the usefulness of such models had its limits. Cornelius Gallus, an important connection of Vergil, is said to have translated works of Euphorion. But that the Greek poet's work exists only in fragments, and Gallus' work in highly *disappointing* fragments, seems significant. Catullus himself, the only one of the Neoteric poets to leave a whole body of work, apparently includes just one direct, close translation of an Alexandrian poem in his collection, "Berenike's Lock of Hair" (Poem 66), a mincing piece of court sycophancy. (A talking — in fact, smarmy — votive offering now turned into a constellation commemorates a consort's devotion to her new husband, warmongering and all.) The Latin poem is an explosive failure; I doubt the original was much better.

What might have been the most practically encouraging thing to the Neoterics about the post-Classical Greek poets was the combination of their solidarity with one another, the support from above that they enjoyed, and their relative freedom and opportunity. The Romantic paradigm is especially badly suited to the lives of ancient authors. No matter how gifted they were, they did not quest boldly and alone from childhood on, suffering and scorned and misunderstood, toward the place where they could deposit the masterpieces they carried in their heads. They wanted to fit in, to have fun, to live among congenial people, and to gain recognition and material rewards for the work they did. For some Roman literary aspirants of the later republic, magisterial Greek libraries and the patronage of Greek rulers during recent centuries projected across the sea a fantasy of a secure literary society, valued for itself and without the heavy demands that Roman households and the Roman state (and the traditional Greek polis too) placed on the time and energy of elites. Apollonius of Rhodes, Nicander, Callimachus, and all the rest were above all *authors,* accommodated as such.

It is in this connection that friendship enters the stage in perhaps the most vital role it played in Vergil's career. The literary friends he made, like Catullus' Neoteric circle, had virtually no institutions at hand besides private libraries to help move them forward. Their literary ambitions clashed with their native method of schooling, their native literature, and the most prestigious native career path, marked by election to a series of increasingly powerful magistracies. But they did have one another, and in quite a dynamic relationship.

The Neoterics may make an impression of rebellion and marginality on us, but they were all upper-class Romans, and at least one, Cornificius, seems to have been an important player in the civil wars. The literary coterie as a whole could not escape being Roman in the old sense, devoted to worldly ambitions far more than to durable aesthetic innovations. But this could work to a born poet's advantage: he could become their headliner. Catullus' unusual talent, however inchoate, evidently mattered to the rest enough for its natural advantages to survive any jealousies of theirs, and in fact for him to win the social support he must have needed and craved while developing that talent. The ancients did not worry as much as we do over the difference between what is practical and self-interested in a personal attachment and what is "sincere" or "real"; they just got enthusiastically on with it (though, as we will see in Vergil's case, that could lead to more trouble in the end).

Octavian's literary circle and the Neoterics probably started out in much the same way, without fixed plans to forward the group or themselves individually, but with a determination to do both somehow. Of course, Octavian was the exception in any group: his ambition was like Abraham Lincoln's as described by his law partner William Henry Herndon: "a little engine that knew no rest." Octavian's political ascendency made a huge difference in the power and reach it lent to his writers, but it could not make the group develop in an unnatural shape. Talented full-time poets turned out to be a minority, whereas the majority were political and military players as well as amateur poets who came to act as literary managers and patrons on the side. They were about as savvy and well positioned as possible to get what they needed out of the authors. But it would not necessarily have been a bad deal for any of them; though more or less traditional patronage relationships manifested (as I discuss in Chapter 4), for Romans on the same educational level, patronage did not exclude mutual respect and practical arrangements to match it.

To try to square the circle, then, of Vergil's character, that of an unusually reticent and withholding man who seems to have been surrounded and cherished even before he delivered the first package of literary goods to his mighty patrons, it might be helpful to consider a poem by Catullus (50) to a member of his literary circle, Gaius Licinius Calvus. Calvus was reportedly an important poet, but the same is reported of many dabblers; he was definitely an orator looming large on the political scene, who repeatedly prosecuted Caesar's henchman the tribune Publius Vatinius. Note the homoerotic language that was common for male Romans in addressing their friends.

> Yesterday, Licinius, a do-nothing day,
> We kept playing with my notebooks —
> Since we'd agreed to pamper ourselves.
> We took turns writing verselets,
> Goofing off, hopping from meter to meter,
> Laughing, drinking as we swapped lines.
> Licinius, I left there on fire
> With your charm, your witty words.
> Wretched, I had no pleasure in food,
> No sleep to cover my eyes in rest.
> In uncontrolled frenzy I tumbled
> Around the bed, lusting to see dawn,
> To speak with you, to be with you again.

(1–13)

To read Catullus' book of 116 poems is to see a world of friendship, a world in which poetry can function at the same time as a language and a forum and a passionate pursuit in itself. Who's cool, who's ridiculous or disgusting, who's talented or a hack, who's in love or lust and how it's going, what other events large or small in the circle need chronicling, what new compositions of insiders or outsiders need heralding or booing. It would be simplistic to write that Catullus depicted his life or that his life inspired him or fostered his work: all kinds of causes, dynamics, and results intertwined and held each other together. But his was a real literary life, not make-believe, with more consequential egos and ambitions supporting it than his own. This was even more the case with Vergil.

I do not base this reconstructive outline merely on the few facts available from Vergil's time and a generation before him. The more copious authors' archives have become over the centuries, and the more detail they show about the years preceding authors' fame, the more they testify to the importance of friendship. Authors as different as Shakespeare, Samuel Johnson, and Zora Neale Hurston had a punishing passage as possibilities for a more conventional life fell away. Shakespeare probably joined a troop of strolling actors (a class of people considered virtual beggars and needing special licensing merely to travel and work), a great comedown from his family's prosperous past. Poverty forced Johnson to drop out of Oxford, and he sometimes walked the streets of London at night hungry. Hurston hinted, with one image years later, that she had literally shacked up with a man on the edge of society. But they all were lucky enough to land early in tight-knit, collaborative groups whose sense of their potential for an outsize contribution brought them confidence and energy, as well as material support.

The first upswing in the fortunes of the humorist James Thurber is my favorite example when I try to reconstruct by plausible analogy Vergil's youthful emergence as a writer. At Ohio State University during World War I, Thurber was blackballed by the fraternities and in danger of flunking out: his off-putting looks and manner, his family's financial struggles, and the military drill, physical education, and science courses he had to deal with in spite of partial blindness created challenges he could not conceivably have met on his own. But the refulgent Elliott Nugent, who was himself to become a Hollywood director, took an interest in Thurber after hearing a comic essay of his read aloud in a literature class. The protégé's ensuing position as fraternity mascot, bard, and theater coordinator led to a number of professional opportunities. Thurber's effusive, hyper-confiding letters to Nugent toy with ways to process abiding resentments and goucheness through words. Nugent's befriending of Thurber also fostered the sociability that eventually made the author congenial to E. B. White and others at the *New Yorker*. Literary achievement, when you consider everything it is up against, is not so much inspiring as preposterous. But most preposterous of all is the idea that an author can make it alone.

CHAPTER THREE

Literary Experiments
and the Literary Lifespan

Modern scholars call the collection of Vergil's putative juvenilia and other experiments the *Appendix Vergiliana,* a title that translates in the obvious way. If it is mostly genuine, it is his own version of Catullus' "little book," a mix of moods, genres, and topics. But scholarly doubt droops heavily over the whole *Appendix.*

I am no expert judge of any poem's authenticity and can only concur with an obvious no in a few cases. What I will mainly do here is take the broadest *biographical* view possible, concentrating on two questions: Is the production of similar groups of works typical of authors? And how could any *Appendix* poems that might be Vergil's fit into our understanding of his experience and character? Admittedly, this second question suggests the argumentative fallacy of begging the question, or mixing up premise and conclusion. If we do not know for sure that Vergil wrote certain texts, what good are they as evidence about the man? But I believe a book about

Vergil's life must be parallel to a lawsuit, whose outcome depends on the balance of probabilities, each of which might have independent evidence, unlike in a criminal case, which demands proof beyond a reasonable doubt and hence solid and closely interlocking claims.

Some of the *Appendix* cannot be genuine. There are two memorial elegies for Vergil's patron Maecenas, who died in 8 BCE, whereas Vergil died in 19. An early collection of the poems even contained two poems by the fourth-century CE Ausonius and one possibly by him; literary collectors do have a propensity to ascribe later and more obscure works to an earlier and greater poet. Also, Suetonius (Life 19) indicates that the authorship of *Aetna*, a work in the Alexandrian style on volcanology, was disputed in his own time; literary credulity did not falter in antiquity without very good reasons.

But should we accept negative critical judgment uncritically? Around the end of the first century CE, Suetonius matter-of-factly lists as Vergil's three collections of short poems and three medium-length poems, two of which he claims Vergil wrote at the age of sixteen (Life 17). These six titles include five in the modern list of twelve representing the *Appendix* as the fullest, most extravagant collection credited to Vergil. And Suetonius, though he is divided from Vergil by several generations, tends to rely on much earlier witnesses. It seems probable that several of Vergil's apprentice works survived, and that they are immature because their author was immature.

In the collection overall, linguistic and stylistic anomalies testify against authenticity. But Vergil was not above odd vocabulary or even mistakes; he would have been much more prone to them when he was young, perhaps having had a late or bungled start in his education, in addition to whatever condition or experience made him a slow and awkward speaker even as an adult. Moreover, genuine Vergilian texts could have been miscopied or deliberately altered later. (All copying was done by hand, and even under the best conditions errors accumulated.) That was naturally more liable to happen when a work did not widely circulate during an author's lifetime, and knowledge, taste, and the language had moved on in the meantime. We have no good reason to believe that Vergil released any poems of the *Appendix* to the general public: Suetonius mentions only that Vergil *wrote* some of them.

A further mark against the *Appendix* has been that Vergil's undoubted works are prefigured there in ways seen as suspiciously thorough and specific. However, this objection defies much evidence in later literary history, including authors' early plans, juvenilia, and late reminiscences. In the area of epic alone, Friedrich Gottlieb Klopstock, the father of German Romanticism, started planning his greatest work, his "Messianic epic," in the equivalent of high school, and when he graduated gave a startlingly advanced oration on epic poetry. In his teens and early twenties, Longfellow covered in minor poems many of the physical and cultural settings of the epics *Hiawatha* and *Evangeline*, and was looking toward their themes. As to specific wording echoed in later works, we do not see much of this now — but modern authors are far less inclined to repeat themselves at that level. Vergil shows a number of evolutions of particularly beautiful and resonant phrasing between poems of his own secure oeuvre. For instance, *Eclogues* 3.60–61 has "From Jupiter [is] the beginning of my Muse: all things are full of Jupiter / He cultivates the land; he cares for my songs," while *Georgics* 2.4–6 has "Come here, Lenaean father [Dionysus], here all things are full / Of your gifts; for you, the field, heavy with the harvest of the vine, / Flourishes." The lines contain not only similar subject matter and vocabulary but also similar meter and word order.

But over time the most persistent and influential argument against the genuineness of the *Appendix* has been that the poems are bad. They seldom reach out to the reader emotionally or aesthetically but instead tend to pedal in eccentric patterns. The Loeb edition of the *Appendix* translated by H. Rushton Fairclough and G. P. Goold — Loebs incline toward the establishment point of view — treats the issue of authenticity this way:

> As was asserted at the outset, it is the greatness of *Eclogues, Georgics,* and *Aeneid* that determines the author Virgil and not the other way round. This consideration enables us to see that the principal question to be asked of the *Appendix* is not so much "Did Virgil compose these poems?" as "Do these poems or any of them reflect or presage the greatness of *Eclogues, Georgics,* and *Aeneid?*"

The Loeb introduction goes on to quote, for a sort of climax of scorn, the great Classicist A. E. Housman:

> The authors of the Culex and Ciris and Aetna were mediocre poets and worse; and the gods and men and booksellers whom they affronted by existing allotted them for transcription to worse than mediocre scribes. The Ciris was indited by a twaddler, and the Culex and Aetna by stutterers; but what they stuttered and twaddled was Latin, not double-Dutch; and great part [*sic*] of it is now double-Dutch, and Latin no more.

This seems a monstrously unfair way to write about ambitious poems packaged together with ephemeral poetic jokes and insults; poems that themselves might have been written collaboratively or even worked on at bibulous get-togethers such as Catullus depicts in his Poem 50. But Vergil does not appear to have had Catullus' precocious egotism, which helped a volume comprising brilliant, not-so-brilliant, and merely quirky or precious poems to survive the author's rather hapless life and early death. Would the modest and cautious Vergil have spent much time on experiments that his instinct told him were not working? Would he have passed them around persistently, so that they were firmly ascribed to him? Or would he simply have put them aside?

A possible scenario in this case is that as the poet grew more famous, people came to hoard any of his early and ongoing discards they could get their hands on, as well as pseudonymous works—the ancient equivalent of fan fiction—and that people in succeeding generations could mis-ascribe texts even more freely. But this does not make it any less likely that a core of genuine but obscure works existed that served as a sort of seed for the production of fakes. Biographically, such a germinating core is strongly suggested. Suetonius shows Vergil on his deathbed bequeathing his works to Varius and Tucca, and stipulating that they publish nothing that he himself had not published or would not have published (Life 40), but he apparently gave no orders to destroy anything but the *Aeneid,* and his hostility (posthumously counteracted) toward his masterpiece would have discredited any hostility he had expressed toward other works.

Pretty much anything seems more probable than that Vergil had no literary apprenticeship. He had little or no personal access to the Neoterics, who belonged to the previous generation, were based in Rome, and concentrated on their own, often idiosyncratic experiments. If he found no one to teach him poetry—or no one to teach him the kinds of poetry that interested him—then his progress would have been all the slower. But it could not have been as fast as modern scholars would have us believe.

The modern evidence of juvenilia makes this all but certain. Authors can trail behind them substantial archives of merely hopeful or disposable work, none of which, from an objective point of view, presages the masterpieces, certainly not in quality, and often not even in type. An aspirant who starts out conspicuously clever may be clever in a very different mode from the later, triumphant one. Flannery O'Connor began her publications as a campus cartoonist, concerned, for example, with the physical presence and looks of the WAVEs training for service during World War II. In Jane Austen's fragment *Evelyn*, exemplary landscaping includes a "paddock . . . perfectly even and smooth, and grazed by four white cows which were disposed at equal distances from each other" — a cute sketch, but at odds with her mature humor.

Moreover, on the ever-increasing evidence, adult literary achievement cannot be augured on the basis of precocity, or ruled out on the basis of slow early development, as achievement is in other fields. Sylvia Plath may provide the most sobering example. She published competent poetry from childhood on but produced most of the poems for which she is best known in a single month, shortly before her suicide at the age of thirty. If the experts could agree on how interesting or uninteresting, how good or bad the *Appendix Vergiliana* is, that still would not prove anything worth proving.

But archives at least frame a general characterization of authors' apprenticeships, revealing the volume of writing these people tend to produce from the time they can read the books they will one day replace. James Thurber, for example, wrote a parody the length of a short book during a period in his life when his most reliable and lucrative outlet was a local newspaper column; he must have known at some level that the parody had no future — with the elasticity that might be the best predictor of publishing success, he gave up trying to market it — but he needed to write it.

Authors as different as Virginia Woolf and Agatha Christie pour ideas, outlines, and passages into notebooks too numerous to keep up with but securely stashed. If Vergil was, as he appears to have been, a modern type of conspicuously isolated author with an independent, obsessive drive to perfect certain literary forms, rather than the typical ancient author who wrote for public occasions and communal edification, then a large archive makes sense. No other ancient writer left schoolboy compositions or later practice sheets that survive, but no other author had a personality or career arc like Vergil's either. Catullus reveals what happened to papers no one bothered to defend: people recycled them as food wrappings (Poem 95). Vergil, I believe, defended his papers and inspired others to defend them.

Of course, if any substantial part of the *Appendix* comes from Vergil, we would be dealing not with the reliable testimony of a secure archive but with scraps left within a powerful political inner circle — according to Suetonius, Varius edited the *Aeneid* for publication (Life 41) — by the premature death of its cultural superstar. To make the situation even more fraught, this superstar had apparently lost his mind, demanding the destruction of his masterpiece. Varius evidently showed considerable respect in his editing of the *Aeneid*, even leaving the uncompleted lines as they were; but would that same respect have extended to Vergil's literary detritus? And what about the next generation of archivists? "Archivists" is of course too formal; these were simply the people who found themselves with the leavings, along with the rest of the physical library.

The case of Sylvia Plath suggests how much license the recipients of a literary estate can feel they have. Her sudden early death left an accumulation of complete but unpublished writings, some arrogantly brilliant, some extremely personal, some shallow and commercial, most immature. Her estranged husband (left with the intestate estate) and others close to him retrieved, repressed, destroyed, edited, and published as it suited them, in spite of protests from the author's enthusiasts. They also wrote and farmed out the writing of highly charged commentary, in effect writing on top of the dead author's work. The ancient world had no cultural basis for resisting, or even noticing, the questionable use of an author's name and unpublished papers.

Innumerable permutations of what might have happened to Vergil's archive are conceivable, but we do not have to accept the *Appendix* as it stands in order to accept what it stands for: a fully human author. The *Appendix*'s comprehensive detractors, I believe, would not claim that Vergil wrote nothing before the *Eclogues* (released in his early thirties); but what they would have to claim instead is that he wrote *another,* much better body of preparatory work but did not keep any of it or let anyone else get hold of it; or perhaps such detractors would claim that his associates had possession of early works but for some reason repressed them all. And this would have taken place in first-century BCE Italy, where even the most private people had no real privacy, where secretaries were part of the normal equipment of writing, and where Vergil was gaining a celebrity unprecedented for a living writer.

Comprehensive detractors of the *Appendix* would also have to explain why imposters did not issue only the forms and content held to be classically Vergilian: Theocritean dialogue between shepherds, for example, or epic battle scenes; and why the pieces were not all in hexameter, the meter of Vergil's three great works. These were the usual ways nameless people stole the authority of famous authors. The *Homeric Hymns,* for example, are all in hexameter, as the Homeric epics are, and the stories are all mythological. *Prometheus Bound* is a phony Aeschylean tragedy, a tale about the gods composed in tragic meters. But the *Appendix Vergiliana* ranges around, as the real, young, unique, experimental author might have.

———

I will not linger on any part of the *Appendix,* all of which may be spurious. But if so, the collection is still a colorful and fascinating literary world that Vergil helped create through his celebrity, and for that reason alone it merits a survey.

Many of the works have suggestive parallels in the Catullan corpus. The *Appendix*'s epyllion *Ciris* (The Sea Bird) and the epyllion that is Catullus 64 are both about the passion of a mythical princess that leads her to betray her father; the keen interest of both authors in female psychology, in apparent imitation of Euripides and Apollonius of Rhodes, may look forward to the portraits of Dido and other women in the *Aeneid.*

In "Lydia," a first-person speaker bewails his separation from his rustic romantic partner, lost along with the land. The poem expands on the *Eclogues* and connects Vergil to the Augustan love poets in giving him a beloved with a three-syllable name that fits into their elegiac meter (closely related to the hexameters of "Lydia"): Catullus had Lesbia, Gallus had Lycoris, Propertius had Cynthia, and Tibullus had Delia, followed by Nemesis. These women were the literary dimensions of real-life company for their lovers' friends as well as their lovers: they were in one sense part of the weave of male friendship. But true to Vergil's discomfort with women, Lydia is no more than a symbol of a heartrending loss, not a believable and memorable personality like Cynthia. In fact, the speaker laments in high-flown but rather confusing terms that he has not had sex with her. Similarly, the women who appear in the part of the *Appendix* called "Slight Poems" (*Catalepton*) are shadow puppets in other men's contemptible intrigues, and bear no resemblance to Catullus' Lesbia, who represented a real woman.

That some of the poems in the *Appendix,* including some of those about Priapus, the magnificently endowed scarecrow god of rape, are bawdy has troubled many worshippers of Vergil. The poet of the *Aeneid*—never! But Roman literary bawdiness was a mode that had its defensible place. Horace's second poem in the first book of his *Satires* teems with crudity. Cicero wrote a long letter about obscenity, arguing humorously that since impropriety exists neither in the word nor the thing, it is nonexistent (*Letters to Friends* 9.22). Vergil himself elides a verb for "had sex with" in *Eclogues* 3.8, but it is clear what the shepherd is talking about. There is no reason why Vergil would not have let 'er rip in a genre appropriate for open lewdness.

The poem "Curses" (*Dirae*), some of the Priapus poems, and some of the "Slight Poems" are in the tradition of attack poetry dating from the pre-Classical Greek period, taken up by a few Alexandrian poets, and received by Catullus with zest. Typical invective is personal if not autobiographical, and "Curses" might follow in this tradition. But the poem is an odd, distanced variation on invective literature, a variation that might suit Vergil's — especially a young Vergil's — dislike of confrontation. A herdsman out of Greek bucolic literature is furious that an anonymous soldier is to have his home ground as a retirement premium. The herdsman thoroughly curses the beautiful land, instead of the soldier himself. The stirring, inside-out take on landscape I discussed in Chapter 1 here amounts to hysteria, as the speaker wishes several incompatible forms of annihilation on his adored countryside.

Poetic rage is uncontrolled here, whereas it is disciplined in the *Aeneid* and elsewhere, but in itself it is a highly Vergilian mode. Moreover, to place the complaint in the mouth of a literary avatar and also deflect the emotion from its true object, as in "Lydia," would have been convenient at a period when the poet's dispossession of his family estate was both unresolved and impossible to treat with clear and direct outrage. In *Eclogues* 9.6, a goatherd curses the new owner of his small plot of land, who is not present, even as he prepares to turn his young goats over to the man; and throughout the poem he and his interlocutor avoid saying anything offensive about the people who decreed the land's expropriation and can rescind it.

"Curses" may be spurious, but then sharp questions loom. Who wrote it, and when, and for what purpose? If it is fan fiction, then it places the original author in an unusually bad light. The specific and agonizing loss that the opening of the *Eclogues* shows Octavian resolving forever is fixed here in livid permanence; the mere ambiguous and threatening situation of *Eclogues* 9 (the dispute over the land is renewed, and some violence has menaced the savior-singer) has a shocking analogy in "Curses": an apocalypse forever invoked out of sheer hopelessness. Would this be a sort of dissident work, like some republican-minded publications of the Neronian period? If so, it is unusual in appropriating Vergil's voice. So far as we know he was not a figure of political dissidence in the ancient world—but, after all, what *do* we know? Overall, it seems most plausible that this was a private expression of Vergil's rage, trotted out long after his and Augustus' deaths, when its political implications were blunted.

Three other longer poems in the *Appendix* do not appear to be beyond arguable possibility of Vergilian authorship. *Moretum* (The Salad) is a recipe embedded in scenes of peasant life. Here the temptation to read in observation, affection, nostalgia, or even experience is great: the protagonist of the poem rises before dawn to make his breakfast, reviving the hearth fire, grinding grain, baking bread, and gathering from his market garden most of the ingredients for a pesto-type relish, which he concocts. He has a female slave, but she gives him strikingly little help. His own hands do all the hard and skillful chores, even going down into the dirt with no tools; as he slowly pounds the vegetables together with other ingredients in a mortar, his eyes, watering from the aromatic fumes released and from the smoke in the room, make him curse. The food is to tide him over during a day of plowing with his bullocks, so his domestic operations end up rather out of focus. A pair of oxen was a costly investment that only a substantial acreage could justify. How can the peasant farm grain on that scale, plus tend the garden and market vegetables, plus do most of the housework?

But this is unliterary niggling. The cinematic detail is remarkable: since Hesiod, writers about rural life had insisted on how hard and hazardous it was. But this poem is a particularly intense depiction of the tedium and the wear of the work—how slowly, for example, the ingredients blend under the pressure of the heavy pestle. Even more remarkably, this is in its essentials a slave's, more precisely a slave woman's, morning: waking before dawn, groping and casting around to organize light and food from materials a step or two away from nature, for the privilege of continuing to work for many more bleak hours. Is this protagonist a mirror image of the happily self-sufficient small farmer of *Georgics* 4.125–146?

In *Copa* (The Hostess), a sexy, drunken, dancing woman encourages her audience to live it up at her establishment. The poem does not approximate Vergil's attitude toward women that all other evidence attests to; this woman is clever but sweet, with tender words even for a traveler's weary donkey. Nor is there any historical evidence that the bad reputation of cookshops, bars, and inns had diminished by Vergil's time. Catullus reviles the "raunchy bar" full of his low-life sexual rivals (Poem 37). The friendly, festive, musical tavern is an institution of a much later era.

In *Culex* (The Gnat), the insect bites a sleeping shepherd to save him from a poisonous snake and is swatted. Thus unjustly consigned to the underworld, the gnat appears later to the shepherd in a dream to complain at great length, more or less exhaustively reprising the traditional lore about Hades. Parody (in this case mainly of pastoral and epic motifs) is a favorite recourse of literary apprenticeship. This poem addresses Octavian as a *puer*, a little boy (26), and this has been taken as a signal of false ascription to Vergil. Octavian was born in 63 and Vergil in 70 BCE, so if Suetonius is right that the work dates "from the author's sixteenth year" (the seventeenth, in our terms), Vergil as a teenager would have been addressing a reverent dedication to a prepubescent boy. If Suetonius is wrong, the reference might partake of playful banter between adults: it is consonant with propaganda that stressed Octavian's youth.

The poem, like *Moretum,* is a convincing enough drill for a young genius. Its pounding stock imagery puts me in mind of an ambitious young pianist's relentless scales and other exercises. Sheer creative will is celebrated topically as well in both *Moretum* and *Culex,* the latter telling about an insignificant creature whose extraordinary action is not so much saving a life through a timely sting as tirelessly memorializing that act, so that he in turn is memorialized. It takes twenty-nine lines for the shepherd to build the mound, plant it with flowers, and set the inscription. The *Aeneid* can take care of that much action in three or four dense, flashing lines like a new blade cutting through all the weedy growth of the poetic past. But sharp expressiveness, like a sharp sword, does not come into being without a lengthy apprenticeship and hard labor.

> With an old man's strength, as far as it allowed
> (But it had overcome a threatening foe in battle),
> He spryly started, by a stream that green leaves hid,
> To give a place an apt shape, planning a circle.
> He turned his staff inventively to new use as a shovel,
> To dig some grassy sod out of the greening turf.

Vergil

His mindful care now followed through the work he had begun,

Massing and heaping much material to make

A monument from earth, within the circle's tracing.

Around he planted stones fashioned from smooth marble,

Attentive to the need for tireless care.

(388–398)

CHAPTER FOUR

Patronage

I n *Satires* 1.6, Vergil's poetic colleague Horace claims that despite being a freedman's son, he deserved adoption into Maecenas' circle: for this aristocratic patron, character counts more than social status. Ironically, however, in this connection character seems to consist mainly of knowing one's place. The poet even avoids alluding to the currency with which he bought Maecenas' notice — talent. Instead, he emphasizes his humble honesty during that first interview. To be considered at all, he had needed a good word from the already ensconced Vergil, and to second Vergil he needed Varius, who was well placed and trusted enough to become one of Vergil's own "literary executors." Nevertheless, it was not until nine months after the interview that Maecenas called Horace back; then, the poet recalls, "You [Maecenas] ordered me to be in the position [rank? category?] of your friends" — or maybe the correct translation is simply "to join your friends" (61–62).

"Ordered" and "friends" are not clashing vocabulary where Roman patronage is concerned. "Friend" in Latin can carry the sense of supporter or ally, as well as someone we would more readily picture as a friend; the word can also mean a patron and perhaps (with this case as an example) a client. The first was the person who granted protection, material help, or other favors to the second in exchange for services that might include organizing his votes when he ran for office. A patron, however friendly, could tell a client what to do. The binding quality of the relationship manifested, for example, in the custom of the freed slave becoming his former master's client and so continuing to serve his interests as a condition of staying free.

But the euphemism "friend" came so naturally as hardly to be a euphemism. The preference not to frame relationships of exchange openly in their pragmatic terms was common in this society. Hence, for example, during the late republic and early empire, taking a fee to defend someone in court was forbidden, so legal advocates (who might be lower in social status but took on for the occasion a patron's protective capacity) would either take fees clandestinely or be owed favors, such as inclusion in a will. But across the board Romans made energetic efforts to give at least the appearance of sincere attachment and comity to patron-client relationships. A crowd of clients gathered at a powerful man's house for the morning *salutatio* (greeting) and accompanied him to the forum or political center of the city. Clients might share a patron's recreations and travels, as well as populating his business and public affairs.

In fact, the word *patronus* is visibly derived from *pater,* the word for "father"; the institution was thus conceptually linked to the lofty Senate (itself named from the word for "elder") with its "enrolled fathers." Patronage had many of the possibilities and limitations of family relationships. Sometimes a patron and client acted as if they were "living together," which is the etymological basis of the Latin word for "dinner party," a Thanksgiving-length performance of social exchange. But *convivia* happened constantly, not once a year. As the first emperor, Augustus staged them regularly, consolidating his various circles, whose goodwill he needed.

But I should not paint too sunny a landscape here. Emotional and social considerations rarely trumped an important man's material interests to the benefit of his dependents. The Roman system was patriarchal, or ruled by fathers, and the *familia* a senior man ruled contained not only relatives but also slaves: the law assigned children and slaves analogous duties of obedience. The "household," or *domus,* was above all a unit organized purposefully from the top, with no quibbling allowed for underlings. This principle shaped patronage, the household projected clear across the public sphere.

Authors could naturally find patronage galling. The satirist Juvenal (who wrote around the end of the first century CE) pities cultured and educated clients of all sorts, half-starved by cynical philistines, and snubbed even by their patrons' slaves (*Satires* 5). But this is well into the imperial period, when Rome had long been exploring the possibilities of synergy between unprecedented power and riches on one hand and on the other an extraordinary flowering of literary talent, when the learning as well as the material goods of the known world poured into Rome. By the late first century CE, however, the possibilities no longer looked open-ended or exciting; it took (for example) a huge fish, a kind never seen before, to rivet the court of the emperor Domitian, as Juvenal narrates (*Satires* 4). According to Suetonius, Vergil could rivet the early imperial court with just a few verses of the *Aeneid.* The poet's description of mourning for the emperor's nephew and potential successor provoked a dramatic reaction by the bereaved mother: Octavia fainted at the lines and was brought around only with difficulty (Life 32).

This was how thrilling and consequential poetry could be at that stage of the empire. And while his masterpieces were still forthcoming, Vergil the impresario was apparently treated as a full and valued human being. Since his eagerly expected services were, to a large extent, part of himself and so could hardly be extorted, he had a very different experience from what Juvenal had or observed.

The wealthy and exquisitely cultured Maecenas was the patron with whom Vergil had the closer and more public relationship, but Octavian as good as owned the whole literary circle, so I will begin with him, trying not to go farther than necessary into his long and complicated political career.

Octavian, who in 27 BCE assumed the title "Augustus," with its suggestions of benevolent, divinely given authority and natural prosperity, was a man of limited cultivation. Though he is said to have been only twelve (eleven by modern reckoning) when he gave the funeral oration for his grandmother, the achievement did not mark him out as a future literary man. Whatever talent he had, he could not have developed fully, as he continued to be marched prematurely onto the public stage and soon took up administrative and military responsibilities. He was a teenager when his great-uncle Julius Caesar chose him as his heir by adoption, and he was still a teenager when Caesar's death left him to avenge and replace his "father." Certain sources suggest that, in a rather pitiful irony, Octavian came no closer to the exclusive rounding out that some of his peers received at Athens than to be deployed, at the time of the assassination, in what is modern-day Albania to oversee preparations for Caesar's planned conquest of the Parthians; his education was the public pretext for sending him there, but a cornucopia of philosophers and rhetoricians could not have been the main part of the experience.

The demands put on him meant that he could not have commanded even a thorough rhetorical expertise, let alone the intellectual ease that his less harried peers had. He managed sometimes to turn the deficit to his advantage, projecting the hard-nosed common sense of a man of action. Still, not to be an author was plainly frustrating for him. Suetonius portrays a man who affected critical taste and literary endeavor but was so anxious that he wrote out and read from not only his speeches to the Senate (memorization of speeches was the custom) but even statements to his wife. He produced some more purely literary works, but only for private audiences, and his poetry was deemed "slight." In writing, he often left out and transposed syllables. His curt, peculiar wit may have been a brilliant man's adaptation to organic blockages in the processing of language.

Vergil, who as a young man showed enough verbal awkwardness to cause doubts about his education and later blended into his work expressions of a lower register than usual for noncomic genres in hexameter, may have been a congenial vicarious genius for Octavian. Both these highly intelligent men operated within a public and literary culture in which verbal facility had immense value. Both were, despite bouts of poor health, conspicuously hard workers and detail hounds. Vergil certainly could not give his chief patron's thoughts a sharper, rhetorically more impressive form, but Octavian did not need that from him. Rather, he needed originality, subtlety, flexibility, and endurance to match his own. No one else in his circle had all these qualities.

Shared social skills supplemented the two men's intellectual similarities. Octavian and Vergil were pragmatists and players of the long game. In Vergil's subordinate role, his greatest friend was restraint, which made him personally unthreatening no matter how intimidating his abilities became. He seems to have let pass without public comment literally volumes of trivial and mean-spirited criticism. Suetonius records a single habitual retort, maybe a private one: that his critics should find out for themselves how hard "stealing . . . a line from Homer" was (Life 46).

A talented author signed on to the service of an authoritarian regime and doing his best to keep his head down offends modern sensibilities, but his historical context urges sympathy for him. I contrast him with Seneca the Younger, who as a tutor and author in Nero's court acquired eye-popping wealth and was close behind the scenes during—if not complicit in—some of the emperor's worst crimes. Augustus was no psychopath, but he disposed freely of people he hated and feared, and his income from confiscations of their property and from legacies nervously left to him was immense. (Vergil himself left him a quarter of his estate [Suetonius, Life 37].) He might have made Vergil a plutocrat; but here is Suetonius on Vergil's demonstrated attitude and the known extent of his enrichment: "When Augustus offered him the property of a man who had been exiled, he could not bring himself to take it. He had nearly ten million sesterces lavished on him by friends, and he had a house at Rome on the Esquiline, near the gardens of Maecenas" (Life 12–13). Augustus may have been the richest person in history; Vergil could have spent all his money acquiring one or two superior mansions in Rome.

Because of Vergil's low-key mode of operating, he would have been invaluable in a regime that above all stressed the avoidance of open competition and conflict. This attitude represented Augustus' prize lesson from the life of Julius Caesar. The notion that a man could be a successful general, a leader of the state, comprehensively learned, and a literary star—and so both deserving of dictatorial privileges and able to extract them by force—had met a predictable death in Caesar. Someone who spread himself so thin, while making himself so conspicuous and so powerful, increased his chances of being brought bloodily down by an elite used to sharing accomplishments and rewards more equally among themselves. A number of senators ganged up and knifed Caesar to death, a collaborative project in contrast to his own way of doing things.

Augustus kept the old power-sharing institutions of the republic functioning, yet under his control, while insisting that his involvement was the minimum essential, and undertaken at the proper authorities' behest. He united the portrayal of the known world's savior and divinely ordained ruler, and that of the adviser and helper — the "first among equals" — to the traditional oligarchy at Rome.

His success as a cultural overlord relied on walking the same kind of narrow line between overreach and excessive caution. His program was very ambitious indeed, but on the literary front he managed — with the expert help of Maecenas and his other literary manager, Messalla, who patronized the love poets Tibullus, Lygdamus, and Sulpicia (the only female author of ancient Rome to have left any poetry that survives) — to balance aesthetics with self-promotion to the degree that surviving works he sponsored are still enjoyable. We can see from Horace's account in *Satires* 1.6 how a potential new recruitment was first delegated down two levels and then considered at length, so few hopefuls got through. (Horace himself gives a cruelly humorous account of a self-recommended applicant in *Satires* 1.9.) We see much less of the management of writers once they were recruited, but that suggests how well the machine ran; writers are not by nature the most discreet group in the world, and the power of the court could not have hidden any ugly goings-on among them: the court could not, after all, repress the evidence of scandals in Augustus' family. Included in what the Augustan circle achieved was a kind of apotheosis of patronage.

This was not the result of some quick thinking on Octavian's part once he was confident of sole rule. Not long after the year 44 at the latest, when Caesar's assassination made him a factional leader, Octavian—perhaps already influenced by Maecenas—thought of cultivating literary talent instead of looking to depend on his own efforts for messaging, as Caesar had in chronicling his own prosecution of the Gallic Wars and an initial round of civil wars (pseudonymous books cover further phases of the conflict). Soon enough to make good use of him after the major victory at Philippi in 42, Octavian consolidated at least a secondhand relationship with a poet seven years older than himself who had withdrawn from public life and from Rome itself, and had produced verses not worthy of his talent—perhaps some of those now extant in the *Appendix Vergiliana;* if not, he had written other works not chosen for his launch into fame.

At some point, Octavian began to bestow all the private investment a substantive literary career in the ancient world required if it was not attached to performances at public festivals or to the law courts. The author Vergil was going to need leisure in an age when even the well-to-do went around in a flurry of business and social activities; he needed a skilled assistant or two or three and a residence that was quiet and retired, away from busy streets with their notorious racket, and he needed either a good library of his own or easy access to other good libraries at a time when books were relatively expensive and difficult to obtain.

If the author wrote something particularly fine, no self-financing media existed to publish or promote it; and before copyright law was dreamt of, he had no prospect of riches from control over its sales. A young author was a worse investment than an unproven racehorse, but money was not even the main problem for Octavian, who inherited enormous sums from Julius Caesar. Imagine an immensely wealthy but still precariously placed young politician buying a three-year-old thoroughbred of no distinguished bloodline and with no wins to his credit. Octavian could not be sure whether Vergil (particularly Vergil) would do him much credit over time, or whether his own successes would continue to justify anyone representing him in a competitive field at all; if not, smug verses about the "god in Rome" like those opening *Eclogues* 1 would blow up in his face.

Nevertheless, the future emperor chose and invested early in the man who would become his foremost poet; Vergil was a monument to Maecenas' taste and Octavian's canny trust in it. But this was Octavian all over. Julius Caesar in his writings shows himself a rapt student of bridge building, siege engineering, naval weaponry, British geography and economics, anthropology of the Germanic tribes — the list goes on. Octavian saved his ingenuity for building sustainable power, through which he could delegate everything else. Whatever he did or delegated reflected back favorably on himself through well-positioned mirrors of communication: inscriptions, speeches, artistic images, building design and siting and use, celebrations, poetry, even the old-fashioned clothing and domestic activities of the women in his family. The mirrors worked so well that they can be considered central to the power strategy, not just an advertisement for it.

Vergil the poet was right there at the fusion of reality and propaganda, among the massive and magnificent public works, the rationalized and flourishing economy, the useful new public services, and peace in most of the known world, all in the emperor's name. But Vergil the author was Augustus' greatest achievement, the most beautiful and the most lasting. The poet's quasi-propagandistic work remains worth reading now that all its ideological and cultural assertions but the most universal have been discredited, at least in liberal democratic nations. Modern ethics reject unquestioning religious, filial, and patriotic "duty," and most especially the divinely decreed "fate" of one race to conquer and rule others. But the *Aeneid* is still running on its *literary* steam.

How did this miracle of a book come about? The peculiar circumstances of the patronage are part of the answer. For a patron to shape and exploit a born author, who is talented to start with and wants nothing more fervently than the means to keep writing, might not seem much of a feat. But then why have other very powerful rulers not been able to pull it off?

One reason is that they do not find their author early enough, or cultivate him intelligently or thoroughly enough, even with cronies or subordinates to guide them. Shakespeare largely made his own way, and he was an established operator before he benefited from Queen Elizabeth's attention; the same for Samuel Johnson before he received a pension through George III. It may be that the rise and reign of Augustus represent a peculiar sweet spot between two kinds of societies. In one kind — that of the ancient Classical world — an author was a fellow citizen or an imported slave, no one to endow with the means to devote his life to art, and no one whose glorification of such a benefactor would be credible anyway; in the other kind — and here we are talking about modern autocracy and plutocracy — such an immense gulf lay between the powerful and the classes from which authors typically come that early discovery and respectful but attentive cultivation were highly unlikely. Maybe the transition from republic to autocracy in Rome, along with the maintenance of the patronage system that eased sociability between a variety of classes, provided the only environment ever suitable for a ruler to raise an author like Vergil to lasting eminence.

So far I have stressed some of the cultural, biographical, and historical background to Vergil's relationship to the Augustan court. But how did that relationship function in the day-to-day world?

The answer is more complicated than we might expect; much more went on than the exchange of political advertising for material support.

Granted, Vergil, with his mania for working to an exquisite standard, might have served well for some years as an agent of decorous political messaging, like a Renaissance court painter who could point himself, or be pointed, at different scenes and scenarios and would hypnotically turn them into unforgettable compositions. Vergil was the only poet at hand whom Octavian could have eventually set to writing a full-length epic poem about the ruling dynasty's purported ancient foundations with the confidence that he would be absorbed in the poem's difficulties and relieve and decorate its necessary heavy-handedness, making it not merely tolerable but a competitor for the title of the ultimate classic. He couldn't help himself.

This is not, however, to say that Vergil and Augustus disagreed on major themes. Sometimes, in fact, Augustus' and Vergil's needs and propensities appear to have met with stunning felicity. Consider, for example, their shared emphasis on youth during their own maturity. Augustus grew up in a hothouse of politics and the military, Vergil in a hothouse of rhetoric, and neither boy could have felt particularly comfortable. Yet each of them made a productive peace with what he could and could not do and turned weaknesses to his advantage.

Augustus did not fret over his stolen childhood and youth but reenacted it as nationalistic fantasy. As he grew older, he continued to issue images of himself looking about twenty-five, often in a general's regalia; though images of him in stately middle age do exist, he never stopped presenting himself as a conquering young god on earth, a statesmanlike Alexander the Great. Other striking emphases on childhood and youth during his regime include bringing the initiation ceremony under his auspices, and issuing moral legislation, a major aim of which was to increase fertility. The secure young family is glorified on the dynastic frieze on the Altar of Augustan Peace (Ara Pacis Augustae), with its rare depiction of small children, realistically distracted and pesky but adequately under the control of patient parents.

Whatever Vergil's childhood and youth were like — and disruption must have played some role in them — childhood and youth coalesced as nationalist ideals in his work, to a degree not evident in any of the other Augustan poets. I have already noted his providential baby in *Eclogues* 4, a child probably anticipated as a peacemaker between political factions and a potential dynastic heir. I also discussed Iulus in the *Aeneid*, who through his name links the Julian clan with his grandmother Venus and is to establish it in Italy after his father's death. He is a virtuoso in all the youthful arts (except slaughter on the battlefield), the precocious born leader, and the sturdy survivor despite his many realistic vulnerabilities; he embodies the future as Augustus himself was purported to. He even serves as a link to the "Troy Game" of horse maneuvers, which Augustus revived and staged repeatedly. Iulus stars in the fictional display, the climax of the funeral games for Anchises in *Aeneid* 5.544–603. What did Augustus's Troy Game look like? How much did it have in common with Vergil's description? It is fascinating to think, that Vergil's passage — or a draft or a plan for a draft — might have been influential. Was this a culture in which a subordinate could shape more than the works of his own expertise? Augustus must have been open to comparisons between the *Aeneid* passage and the real cavalry choreography.

Augustus always worked with what he had, and he deployed his literary coterie with a boldness and subtlety suitable to the delicate circumstances of the early empire. In line with his usual resistance to whatever might smack of Eastern despotism, Augustus did not set up a true literature of the court. There was no known central gathering place or workplace like the libraries of Antioch and Alexandria; the library that Asinius Pollio founded was a *public* library, without showy special facilities for sponsored writers. There was no importing of talented men from distant lands to turn into major figures, though Roman leaders had done this in the past and would do it in the future. There was no competition for public posts such as librarianships for writers, or grants for them from public funds; the authors' support came from a diffuse private network. Although the resources that Augustus caused to be channeled to individual writers may have made the greatest of the Ptolemies look cheap, he always had deniability about the connection between what authors were paid and what they wrote.

And this deniability found further support in the appearance of comity and good humor among the dependents and those they depended on. Horace's memory of his own youthful forelock-tugging in front of Maecenas is not typical; elsewhere he dramatizes what good friends make up the circle. He plays the moral adviser and philosophical wag to prominent named addressees; stages a seriocomic conversation about literary libel with his pal the renowned legal expert Trebatius Testa (*Satires* 2.1); issues an invitation to a plain, hearty rustic dinner at his own place to a man named Torquatus (*Epistles* 1.5), probably a member of a prominent family; aims special literary and intellectual flattery at Julius Florus, a friend of Tiberius, Augustus' eventual heir; and shares no end of amusing gossip with well-known acquaintances.

Moreover, literary celebrations of Augustus tended to be contextualized in the larger religious and civic traditions he presided over, enhanced, revived, or claimed to revive. Horace's "Song of the Ages," performed chorally at the Secular Games in 17 BCE, is a pious and patriotic hymn, invoking general blessings (but especially those of fertility and the protection of the young). Roman victory in battle, the military Triumph procession with its exotic captives, other Roman festivals and rites within the compass of the state religion — these are all set-pieces of Augustan literature, including Vergil's works, but the glory tends to shine on Rome generally; the leader's appearances usually remain within harmonious proportion.

The emperor's relative propagandistic modesty in the literature he sponsored, given that he also claimed to be divinely descended and a god himself and set up his own worship throughout the empire, is naturally confusing — but it would not have been so to the Romans. Their universe was infused with divinity, and they almost never drew lines of separation between the natural and supernatural worlds. The gods had many offspring and elevated whomever they wished to heaven. But kings were anathema to Rome. Augustus needed above all to avoid a despot's uncontextualized self-glorification; his authors helped by placing him amid all kinds of things, superlative and ordinary and even trivial.

The new kind of literature that Augustus promoted was not moralistic or patriotic in its main tenor, let alone focused on his particular goals. Horace himself, who was eventually to write the bombastic "Roman Odes," usually comes across as a canny everyman or a literary or philosophical village explainer. Of the extant Augustan authors, only Livy is a Roman patriotic warhorse, but not even he was an efficient propagandist. He updated the genre of annalistic history that necessarily focused its idealism on the centuries-long development of the republic, with its many glorious heroes, including the legendary first Brutus, who helped overthrow the last king, Tarquin the Proud, and was claimed as an ancestor by the Brutus who played a leading role in plotting Caesar's assassination.

Love elegy, with its three great Augustan practitioners, Propertius, Tibullus, and Ovid, drew on Greek models, and its woman-centeredness was far from traditionally Roman. The elegists, especially Ovid, favored humor and irony. Only on its own terms did this literature, reflecting the pleasant, secure private life, the mind and body's *chosen* occupations, celebrate the new era of peace and prosperity. Love elegy even got away with focusing on the demi-monde and cheekily embracing the "military service of love," with the lover "camping out," shivering, on the doorstep of his cruel mistress.

A great deal of Vergil's own *Eclogues* is poetic soap opera, often implying (as does Theocritus' *Idylls,* its source) that shepherds had nothing better to attend to than their courtships and singing competitions. Only in the *Georgics* does Vergil begin to stress the demands of the land itself and the rustic virtues that made "Rome the most beautiful thing in the world" (2.534). The idea is critical to the main subject matter and themes of the poem and to its aesthetic integrity; praise of Octavian and Maecenas absolutely is not.

To reconstruct how, in the most practical ways, Vergil and his work could have fit into the literary environment, it seems useful to look first at its strange makeup in the early years, when the boundaries between statesman, military man, or politico (or some combination of these) and poetic dabbler or aspirant were often blurred. In this way I can at least show by contrast what Vergil as a professional poet was not like and did not do.

As a young student of Latin literature, I learned about high-level operators on Octavian's behalf, associates of Vergil who were also poets themselves. A professor would occasionally lament, on the grounds of Vergil's and others' praise, that someone's writings had not survived. But two persons provide a wider scope for commentary, both because they appear to have been important connections for Vergil and because some of their own work is extant.

The first is Gaius Cilnius Maecenas, an able diplomat and fixer who was also a wealthy cultural showman, with famous gardens and the assignment of cultivating Augustus' most important poets. Maecenas had literary ambitions himself, but the preciousness of his expression was linked to his effeminacy and excessively luxurious lifestyle. He eventually fell from Augustus' favor, for reasons that may have included the regime's embarrassment. Manliness ranked high among the Roman virtues (the word *virtus,* from which "virtue" derives, literally means "manliness"). The emperor was anxious to put it out — especially through his poets — that the last rivals he had defeated were a eunuch-like cohort led by a woman, Cleopatra. The consequences for Vergil, with his pronounced homoerotic disposition and his close personal ties to Maecenas, were probably substantial.

The second most conspicuous associate was Gaius Cornelius Gallus, who became prefect of Egypt but committed suicide after his arrogant behavior triggered his recall in disgrace. Scholarly excitement at a newly discovered papyrus showing parts of a poem by Gallus gave way to much sighing and rolling of eyes. The work includes a toadying address to Octavian and an apparent declaration to his mistress that he has nothing to fear from critics as long as she approves his verses. The nakedly personal element in both the provincial leadership and the poetry, similar to the element of Maecenas' effeminacy, speaks to these two men's exposed roles: Here I am, energetically being my very noticeable self in relation to the ruler, you. Maecenas was, presumably, in front of the emperor's eyes in his outré outfits. Gallus writes, "My fate will be sweet to me, Caesar, / When you prove to be the greatest part of Roman history." But he then seems to present himself as subordinating his work, presumably including this very pose, to a woman's judgment, doubling up on the kind of self-abasement that makes the

self even more obtrusive. These are the antics of a disposable courtier, unless the ruler's judgment is pretty far gone.

What did Vergil do that was different to serve the needs and
demands of the regime credibly and durably? He was surrounded
by career politicians who did not all stay in the action, though staying in the action was the main point of their lives.

Vergil's writing makes up by far the bulk of the evidence. The
trickiness of the required balance — between commitment and
deniability, between flattery and self-respect, between literature
and propaganda — is evident even in the pre-imperial *Eclogues*. *Eclogues* 1 (with its follow-up, *Eclogues* 9) probably refers to events in
the aftermath of the Battle of Philippi in 42. A biographical reading
of the poem's opening would convey that Vergil's family farm was
confiscated but then given back because of the political influence
he could command, whereas his neighbors lost their land permanently and tragically. One herdsman, Tityrus, is sitting in the shade
happily piping a love song, to the chagrin of a refugee, Meliboeus,
who passes by with his suffering and doomed flock amid the general upheaval of the countryside. The lucky Tityrus explains that a
"god" secured him a carefree livelihood.

But soon the poem seems to start over, after two jarring bumps.
Asked who this god is, Tityrus merely dilates on the overwhelming
size of Rome. Asked for the reason he went to Rome, he responds
in Theocritean terms, far removed from politics and history: he has
gained his freedom from slavery thanks to his change in partners.
It is clearly implied that with Galatea managing his affairs, he could
not save enough to buy himself out of bondage; Amaryllis took
over, and now he looks forward to a life of serene prosperity. Meliboeus makes further complaints about his exile and enviously pre-
dicts Tityrus' enjoyment of the land, and Tityrus pours out further
thanks to his benefactor; but the images of nature are all so quaint

and literary that they render the political allusions interspersed with them quite jarring. This is not the worst incongruity in the poem. Tityrus' U-turn to the topic of manumission makes it sound as if the "god" he had never seen before manumitted him. But Romans reserved the power of manumission for the slave's master; it was an ancient and basic prerogative. Tityrus' former master is not mentioned in the poem.

The bulk of the *Eclogues* is firmly Theocritean, showing an almost self-enclosed set of pastoral masquerades, with contemporary Roman names thrust in like American political jokes in a modern staging of an Aristophanes comedy. The only eclogue that is arguably political as a continuous whole is the fourth. It somewhat resembles Near Eastern poetry celebrating the birth of an heir to a dynasty; this would be the nephew Octavian could have acquired through the marriage of his sister to Mark Antony. (The couple instead had two girls.) But the poem's subtlety in expressing this political inspiration—Christian readers were to maintain that Vergil was heralding the birth of Christ—suggests that Octavian did not have the power, or did not have the desire, to have himself and his ambitions promoted blatantly.

Others in Vergil's circle teeter on the edge of absurdity as they appear in the *Eclogues*. True, politically powerful amateur poets are mentioned by name and with a surface fervor. Vergil dedicates *Eclogues* 8 to Pollio, who is returning from a stint as a provincial governor; he had in fact won a military victory, earning a Triumph. Vergil elastically writes that he longs to celebrate both what Pollio has done and what he has written—tragedies worthy of Sophocles. The wild flattery is cheap, as the full tribute, of course, never happens. In *Eclogues* 9:32–36, Vergil speaks through the mouth of a tuneful shepherd to confess that though the Muses have made him a poet and other shepherds call him a divinely inspired one (literally, a "prophet"), he does not trust the shepherds (or possibly the Latin refers to both the shepherds and the Muses): he has not done anything worthy of Varius or Cinna — yet; he only honks like a goose among the shrill swans. The dismissive treatment of the Muses themselves, the bestowers of his gift, sounds like a laughable degree of humility, and the "yet" is heavily weighted: Vergil is about to move on to a more ambitious genre, didactic poetry, where he will not mention any contemporary poets as such.

An important lieutenant of Octavian, Gallus, takes up the entire tenth and final eclogue but in the manner of pastoral burlesque, as a lovesick suicidal poseur. Gallus gets the royal rural treatment: like his model Daphnis in Theocritus' *Idylls* 1, he is bewept by all nature, and gods associated with the countryside attend to him. But whereas Daphnis is, without further comment from the poet, surrounded by sorrowing cattle (74–75), Vergil's concerned sheep come with an ironic dig: "Around him sheep stood too. They don't find us objectionable — / Don't find the flock objectionable, godlike poet"; even the lovely Adonis was a shepherd (16–18). Vergil slides from Gallus' emotionally extorted ovine entourage to his own demand for Gallus' regard for a piece of pastoral literature, and he means this new collection of poems itself. The man who wrote it could not fail to know that it was better than anything yet written in his generation.

The coda to *Eclogues* 10, plausibly representing the first-person voice of the author, ends the group of poems and characterizes them as a tribute to Gallus.

That's enough singing for your poet, Pierian Muses,
As he sits plaiting a small basket from fine mallow stems.
It's you who'll make these things the biggest for Gallus;
My love for Gallus grows every hour, as much as at the start

Of spring the greening alder tree rises hour by hour.

Let's get up: the shade tends to weigh heavily on singers;

Juniper shade weighs down; shade hurts the crops too.

You're fed full, she-goats: go home; go, as the Evening Star comes.

(70–77)

Here the irony sounds truly heavy-handed. The first line suggests a limit to dues paying by a poet who, after all, belongs to the Muses, not to a single poem's subject. The speaker then shows himself weaving a modest basket, though presumably with skill and from flower stems that are "fine," or "slender" or "gracefully subtle," according to the Alexandrian metaphor for the right kind of poetry. The Muses will make his work "the greatest" or "the biggest" for Gallus — ambiguous wording; big poetry is bad poetry by the Alexandrian standard. And what does it mean to make something the biggest "for" someone? In his eyes? In competition with him, since he is also a poet? The possibility of homoerotic humor cannot be dismissed here either. The very vagueness of the "big things," along with the "love" (*amor,* which can be an erotic term) that grows inexorably bigger, as the alder tree does in the season of fertility, is suggestive. Vergil's egregious flattery might have become louche, focused not on Gallus' scrolls any longer but on his body. But in these poems (very much unlike in the poetry of Gallus that we know), nothing is one thing only.

Another indication of negativity and withholding is that the idyllic shared day is drawing to a close. The shade threatens the singers, and the crops too; the *Georgics* will repeatedly mention the dangers of shade to crops. But the speaker hurries his goats — creatures that in reality do benefit from shade — anxiously away home, as if both he and they have had their fill of this outwardly pleasant scene of poetic collegiality; something in it that he knows about but we do not is unpleasant, and he is better off on his own.

Yet Gallus, if Suetonius' account is correct—though biography could well have been read in from literature in this case—was one of the poet-politicos (Pollio was the other) who intervened to save Vergil's farm for him at the time of the confiscations. It would not have been a favor for which Vergil could thank anyone baldly and directly; certainly not in the Second Triumvirate's transitional circumstances, and certainly not according to the culture of messaging that Octavian was setting up. He *could* praise fellow poets, but he knew how ridiculous this was, given the differential in talent. Did they?

Vergil's at best over-the-top or self-undermining puffing of his amateur colleagues in the *Eclogues* reminds me a little of the social and emotional reciprocation that the "anti-Callas" Florence Foster Jenkins, a well-insulated socialite and patron of music, received from such luminaries as Cole Porter and Enrico Caruso while she made an unwitting bid for the status of worst singer of all time. Zora Neale Hurston, however, is my prize winner for an unnoticed (or unacknowledged) putdown of a patron who set herself up as a competitor. Hurston addressed to Charlotte Osgood Mason, whose demands for control of Harlem Renaissance writers reminded them why they had fled the South, a parody of the Nativity in which the glorious whiteness of the newborn Mason foretold her beneficent destiny to her awestruck parents.

Still, as Hurston found, the game can be consequential to a dire degree. Writers must maintain helpful relationships, even if the cost is high. Among many modern examples is that of the sickly Robert Louis Stevenson's nearly killing himself with an Atlantic voyage and a cross-continental American train ride in order to finally secure the older woman he knew would be the wife, nurse, organizer, and fellow adventurer able to promote him from dilettante to literary star. And he made a number of uncongenial and artistically compromising concessions to her wishes, including fostering her mediocre writing.

But if Vergil needed Octavian and his cronies in this way, they also needed him. The poet knew he had power of his own, and could offer work like the tantalizing cut-and-paste *Eclogues* 1 while pledging to keep working and improving — *if* conditions were right for nurturing his abilities. Horace's memory of Vergil in the "Journey to Brundisium" satire points to a situation like this. (Brundisium, modern Brindisi, was the city where Octavian negotiated a peace treaty with Antony in the year 40 — that is, a year or two before the *Eclogues'* publication.) The aspiring poets cannot escape their duty to join Octavian during his important diplomatic conference, though they will play no direct role in it. Horace sardonically describes the expedition's hardships and irritations: loud, maudlin singing that keeps travelers awake, a fiery accident in a kitchen, scores of other things he could have done without. Vergil joins the travelers later, in the company of a couple of notables (Plotius and Varius); Horace's words for the joy of the meeting do not specify whose joy it was. Vergil is only momentarily visible from then on, retiring from an evening ballgame because of stomach trouble while Horace retires because of his bad eyes. Was Horace's own privilege of begging off on this occasion activated by the presence of his more privileged friend?

After Octavian defeated his main rivals through the Battle of Actium and follow-up actions, Vergil (according to Suetonius) recited the *Georgics* to him. Octavian's collaborator Maecenas is named in the poem's second line; Vergil invokes him even before invoking the gods presiding over the various natural and agricultural realms the poem will describe. From line 24, however, he turns to Octavian (under the name of Caesar), explicitly referring to the Julian clan's claims of divine ancestry as he looks forward to Octavian's deification. *This* god will preside anywhere he chooses in the universe, and, plainly, he already outweighs all the others in authority and beneficence: he must accustom himself to farmers and their poet praying to him to favor their tasks. At the end of book 1, Octavian figures as the savior of agricultural Italy from the horrors of the wars that are raging throughout the world.

Most of the long passage opening book 3 is devoted to Vergil's vision of presiding in his own home district over various celebrations and commemorations of Octavian's victory. Turning then to the subject of herd and work animals, he states that Maecenas has laid this difficult and lofty task on him (40–45); but in the next few lines Vergil makes a conventional promise to compose poetry about Octavian's battles in the near future. The *Georgics'* last lines, closing off the story of Orpheus and Eurydice, testify that the poem was written while Octavian was achieving dominion in eastern realms and "aspir[ing] to the road to Olympus."

But such outpourings do not fit well into the structure or subject matter of the poem as a whole. As with the *Eclogues,* there is no sign that the author wrote with politics or even people foremost in his mind. Vergil could have plausibly been laboring for years on this second poem of personal importance to himself, with its topic of country life, and he could have inserted his tributes later. Indeed, their tone is at odds with all the moving and believable characterizations of the country as a world apart, which new national leadership could not fundamentally alter: life on the land will remain hard, intermittently satisfying, and chancy.

But, as already noted, one striking difference of the *Georgics* from the *Eclogues* is a great narrowing and rationalizing of the flattery doled out, as if the author is now free to abandon the poses of poetic parity, collegiality, and even subordination that suit the dialogue structure of several eclogues and the overarching theme of poetic performance. This turning away from the poetic coterie endows his own voice with much greater authority. Even the previously celebrated Gallus is off the stage here. Many experts doubt Vergil's late-fourth- and early-fifth-century commentator Servius in his report that, with Gallus now fallen from Octavian's favor, the "praises of Gallus" had to disappear from the *Georgics'* final portion; the Orpheus and Eurydice narrative is supposed to be the substitute. (Servius probably mixed the *Eclogues* and the *Georgics* up. This is not as far-fetched as that Gallus was set to overshadow both Octavian and Maecenas in a poem explicitly dedicated to them.) But in any case, the story of (Aristaeus and) Orpheus and Eurydice, taking up 278 lines of book 4, which is only 566 lines long, throws the entire poem magnificently off track.

The story is an operatic flight, which could well have started as a separate poem, an epyllion; with its theme of obsessive and destructive romantic love, it could have been a companion to *Ciris* in the *Appendix Vergiliana.* It contains some of the most gorgeous lines in literature, such as the depiction of dead souls in the underworld gathering, a mass of obscure, helpless remnants of tragedy as thick as birds fleeing evening darkness or a winter rainstorm (471–477). The most memorable part, about Orpheus himself, is neither traditional nor edifying, as befits a didactic poem on agriculture; it surrounds the figure of the singular artistic genius with otherworldly glory and doom. The tale's insertion here, with only a flimsy connection — Aristaeus' role as a beekeeper — to the section's stated subject of bees, looks confident to the point of insolence. The end of the *Georgics* thus places Vergil on an upward poetic arc that is largely self-expressive. Octavian was probably in accord, or at any rate unable to apply effective pressure for something different, in spite of financial outlays for the poem that he had made or endorsed.

But the upward trajectory had inherent perils. For one thing, it was isolating. The amateur poets were, in their identity as poets, claiming far less written attention from Vergil. (They had probably never claimed much attention through their own writings.) But the biographical tradition suggests that some of them, in moving out of the quasi-collegial position, took up roles as Vergil's caretakers and minders — roles that could turn toward taskmastering and spying, especially during the final years of the poet's life. Here Varius is most interesting. He was clearly not a poetaster or a dabbler but a productive and well-regarded epic and tragic poet. He appears at the beginning of Vergil's career, mentioned in the *Eclogues,* and he was there after the end, as a "literary executor." As I discuss in the next chapter, he was there in the meantime, performing services such as offering the poet a courtesan. But his own work survives only in fragments. These facts encourage me in the conviction that the more interest Vergil generated in his own work, the lonelier he was. How could he trust and confide in fellow authors he was so devastatingly out-competing?

In other ways too, the passage of time proved unfriendly to Vergil. A late, laborious developer, he slowly provided work of increasing beauty and depth, but by the stage, sometime during the *Aeneid*'s composition, when it became clear that he would not in the future write anything better than this work, or anything better suited to the new regime's needs, or anything more at all, he would have found the thought of outliving his leverage harrowing. The perfectionism that kept his progress slow had a companion motivation: each episode of the epic he handed over represented months of the privileged conditions he could claim he needed for composition. A chosen, congenial lifestyle was moving off the ledger of his future.

He could not look forward to an ordinary retirement, because Augustus was on an autocrat's usual trajectory of increasing grandiosity, overwrought expectations, and irascibility. His very determination to project moderation and reasonableness may have built up reserves of rage to be let out when someone he had given latitude disappointed him; it was naturally worse in the case of those he trusted and depended on the most to protect and enhance his reputation and perpetuate his dynasty. He savagely punished his daughter and granddaughter, the two Julias, for sexual derelictions, but they must have had considerable freedom initially in order to pursue their intrigues. Augustus suddenly exiled Ovid, a poet in the generation after Vergil, to an outpost on the Black Sea and let him die there, ignoring years of his versified pleas to be allowed to come home. In short, Augustus was vindictive, and his revenges became worse over time. That Vergil did not live to see the worst did not mean that he failed to see it coming.

A passage of the Suetonius biography seems to concur with this scenario by representing two stages of Vergil's career in relation to the emperor's moods.

> Virgil read the *Georgics* to Augustus out loud for four days straight, as
> Augustus was spending time nursing his throat in Atella, on his way
> home after the victory at Actium; Maecenas stepped in and took a turn
> at reading whenever the poet's voice wore out, causing an interruption.
> In any event, his delivery was sweet and uncannily seductive. . . .
>
> Even when the poem was barely started, the reputation of the
> *Aeneid* was such that Sextus Propertius did not shrink from announcing

this: "Fall back, Roman writers, fall back, Greeks: / Something greater
than the *Iliad* is being born" [*Elegies* 2.34.65–66].

In fact Augustus (who happened to be abroad on an expedition
in Cantabria) wrote to Virgil with entreaties, but also with threats, in
a humorous letter to demand that he send him (and these are his own
words) "your preliminary submission [*hypographe:* the term is in
Greek, and was originally a legalistic one] of the *Aeneid,* or any convenient *colon* [a Greek word for part of a line of verse, a clause of a sen-
tence, or a line, fragment, or snatch of a literary work]." At last, much
later, when Vergil had polished his material, he recited a total of three
books for Augustus: the second, fourth, and sixth. (Life 27–32)

Maecenas is shown making up for Vergil's physical limitations in
a public role, by acting as a fellow performer of the *Georgics;* this
accords with Horace's portrait of the patron as a sympathetic friend
and intellectual companion. But Vergil's own voice was so charm-
ing that the cultural cupboard was well stocked in the first place.

Yet when a poem more beautiful and important and germane
to his purposes was pending, Augustus grew impatient. The epic
Aeneid places on a Homeric level of prestige and elaboration the
legend of refugees from the Trojan War settling in Italy, and firmly
links the divine descent and lofty destiny of their leader, Aeneas, to
Augustus' own; through these two men above all others, the history of the world culminates, and the world's future is assured, in
the glory of Rome.

What was in the letter the patron sent his client, besides con-
descending irony? What kind of threats did he convey, and how
funny were they to their target? Cicero wrote to a historian in an
effort to manipulate him into producing an extremely favorable
account of an episode in the orator's career (*Letters to Friends* 5.12).

Did Augustus work on Vergil in similar ways, only harsher, in proportion to his greater power? And did it not occur to Vergil that when Augustus had what he wanted, he would react against its creator, who had given him so much trouble extracting it? A sense of the ominous could have added to more ordinary motivations for poetic coyness in drawing out the period of composition.

In any event, the biographical tradition seems to show Vergil getting away for some time with being the poet of his own vision and not overexerting himself to promote the new regime. As with the *Eclogues* and the *Georgics,* he could have repurposed for the *Aeneid* material that was conceived with nothing but literature in mind; perhaps he used up much of this material before dutifully shaping a more edifying story as a whole. True, one part of what Suetonius claims Vergil recited, the end of *Aeneid* 6 (a book that is mainly an epic *nekuia* or journey into the underworld, but with Alexandrian-style elaboration), provides a hyper-patriotic take on Roman history and an affecting lament for Augustus' heir apparent. But the village of Pallantium, with its noble inhabitants as a rough draft of Rome, and Vulcan's shield, which shows Roman history culminating in the Battle of Actium (with the young god-general at the center of it), are reserved for book 8, and so would not have been in this early tranche; the rest of the recitation, books 2 and 4, are, respectively, an Odyssean account of magical travel adventures and (mainly) a Euripidean tragedy or Neoteric epyllion, which was to set romantics down the generations rooting for Dido, a female embodiment of Rome's arch-enemy, Carthage. If Augustus wanted a big slice of promotional meat, and a minimum of artsy garnishes and fluffy creative risotto, in the starter course he hungered for, he did not get it.

On the whole in the *Aeneid,* sustained and explicit patriotic material is rare outside books 6 and 8, and ironies, ambiguities, and even protests abound. And the more ambivalent and scarifying of the "war books" (a designation for the second half of the twelve-book-long *Aeneid*) — 7 and 9 through 12 — preclude the enshrinement within them of Augustus, a leader more or less glued to images of victory, peace, and prosperity. The gloom of the *Iliad* and its heroes' narrow view of the world prevail here, and the breakdown of the hero Aeneas into murderous and vengeful fury in the final lines is notorious.

As I have argued, Augustus' frequent efforts to depict himself as a mere adviser to the elite and a fatherly protector of the state are consonant with poetry that did not look strained or meretricious, like the work of courtiers. But this does not mean that the restraint he showed toward his author-clients stayed easy over time, or without exceptions earlier than Ovid's banishment. He was an autocrat by instinct, and increasingly in reality and by habit. His appetite for praise bursts out like a paunch from a corset in *The Achievements of the Divine Augustus*. A divergence in interests between him and Vergil was inevitable, and it would worsen over time.

CHAPTER FIVE

Love and Art

In Suetonius' biography, some gossipy dilation on Vergil's erotic inclinations follows an account of his appearance, health, and eating habits. An ancient author could discuss an important man's sex life freely, at least at safe distances of time or space from him. Caesar's reputation never got over a youthful homosexual indiscretion (or just the rumor of it), and Suetonius happily passes on dirt even about past emperors. Here he presents Vergil as a sexual personality.

> He was unusually prone to infatuation with boys, and he was especially
> fond of Cebes and Alexander, whom he calls Alexis in the second poem
> of his *Bucolics* [*Eclogues*]. This boy was given him by Asinius Pollio.
> Neither boy lacked cultivation, and Cebes was actually a poet. The
> rumor spread that he also had cohabited with Plotia Hieria. But
> Asconius Pedianus maintains that she herself used to say in the pur-
> ported aftermath, when she had reached her later years, that Vergil
> was invited by Varius to have a relationship with her, but stubbornly
> refused. There is no doubt, anyway, that in other realms of his life he

was so proper in speech and thought that at Naples he was commonly called "Parthenias," and that whenever he appeared in public in Rome — seldom as he went there — he would run off to the nearest house to get away from people who followed him and pointed him out. (Life, 9–11)

The notion of Vergil as a pederast would not in itself have shocked the Romans. His sexual partners register as his own or his friends' slaves or other dependents, all of whom would have been sanctioned sexual outlets. A regular such outlet could be a household fixture, his function known to guests, other slaves, and the master's family. I do not believe that Vergil was actually in the romantic position of the herdsman Corydon, the main voice of *Eclogues* 2, who hopelessly pursues his master's "favorite," Alexis; a slave had no right to refuse the master or the master's stand-in, but he would refuse the master's subordinate rival if he knew what was good for him. In the seriocomic fluff of pastoral poetry, this is a love triangle of sorts. In reality, Vergil was the owner or controller of his erotic objects, so any drama of pursuit and frustration would have been minimal.

There is no sharper divergence in morals between the Christian and pre-Christian worlds than in the "use of boys." In translating Catullus 56, scholars tend to skate around the full brutality, but it is there. The poet gloats for four lines in a prelude to a "too-hilarious" incident that his friend needs to know about: he has caught a "little tyke" having sex, and, "may it please Diona [= Venus]," he "slew" the boy, using his "rigid [a word for the penis is elided] as a spear." The incident may be made up or exaggerated, but the mere language is beyond the pale for us. There was, however, a prevailing moral logic behind the poet's attitude. If he preyed sexually on someone defenseless and did not take the act seriously, then his own independence of mind and the conventional ranking of his priorities in life would remain undisturbed, whereas the effort, suspense, and frustration accompanying an actual love affair would upset them. As Catullus experienced, and showed in his poetry, an adult lover with a mind of her own, especially if she were an elite Roman too, and married, could mean serious embarrassment if not dangerous entanglement. (Catullus' "Lesbia" has been identified as Clodia, a consul's wife, whom Cicero vilified as he defended one of her former lovers against several charges, including murder.) Passing sexual encounters and sexual relationships of convenience had a purported ethical function in providing a physical release and allowing a man to return wholeheartedly to his duties.

The Platonic angle, the idealization of impulses that were basically pederastic, also manifests. Suetonius approvingly asserts that both the named boys were cultivated, as if they appealed to Vergil more for this reason or had picked up some learning from him. Plato saw an older lover with the right attitude as a beneficent influence on the object of his desire, whose beauty could elevate the lover's soul and inspire him to become a restrained guide and a moral influence for the long term. (Someone added to the Donatus version of this passage the opinion among "good men" that Vergil's love for boys was chastely Platonic; this whitewash tries to cover the original clear implication that the boys were catamites.)

The modern impulse is to call Pollio and Varius procurers (or a less polite term). Romans would have seen them as managerial patrons or thoughtful friends, bestowing a congenial boy and offering the services of a courtesan the way they would urge the best dishes on an honored guest. Vergil does appear to have been a sort of perpetual guest, even, in a sense, on properties he owned. Others looked after concerns (the choice of erotic "favorites," for example) that normally fell to the head of a household.

The tendency to hold himself apart and stay at least periodically on the move must have been in part a function of his sexuality as he experienced it in a fairly unwelcoming culture, one that cast a shaming light on a man who did not fill prescribed manly roles, especially those of husband and father. The information we have places Vergil on the far homosexual end of the Kinsey scale — like Plato himself, who also appears never to have married, despite the rigidly normative status of marriage. The single anecdote about Vergil's sexuality creates a rather awful scenario: the courtesan evidently took some time to accept his resistance to her popular charms, increasing the awkwardness. (Imagine if the Christmas gift that goes to the charity shop the next week could object.) No wonder Vergil avoided the sexual confrontations a wife, a girlfriend, or ordinary female prostitutes would have brought with them.

Horace never married either, but unless he was a very good liar and his friends and the gossips at large conveniently unobservant, the younger poet did not lack the exuberant and adaptable appetites that Romans thought were a sign of a real man. This attitude was inevitable in a society with military expansion built in. Rome sponsored a huge, war-based slave trade; looting — including the looting of human beings — was a sanctioned, regulated benefit for men all the way up from the new legionary recruit to the official who combined the functions of general and governor. Roman men *took*. But Vergil reads like anything but a violent taker, indifferent to the feelings of the taken. Besides the personality Suetonius describes, he never saw military service. This alone would have made him an odd man out in the late years of civil war. (Even Horace with his humble origins was recruited for the republican side and given the high rank of legate.) Though Vergil had sexual prerogatives he could exercise, I cannot imagine him as a sporting, boasting, sexual opportunist.

The "Slight Poems" section of the *Appendix Vergiliana* reinforces my impression of the opposite: "Vergil" is a defensive, sharp-tongued observer of others' antics. In Poem 13, he aims particularly vicious taunts at the "woman" who has impugned his manhood because he is not up to the active military life "any longer": this person's own buttocks have dripped with semen at orgies, and he performs servile cunnilingus on a detested, fat wife. The poem sounds like typical lashing out by a sexually insecure man. More honest sounding is Poem 7: the poet jokes to Varius that that damned Desire (here a Greek word) has done him in; if it is not proper to say that, then that damned boy (a Latin word) has done him in. Admitting a child's or youth's power over him is fine, but using a foreign word in Latin poetry is not. Catullus, in contrast, is confident enough to attach the plausible authorial "I" to real pain and damage at the hands of a love object, pain and damage not to be passed off as a joke. Neither Vergil nor pseudo-Vergil ever expresses himself in this way.

All the evidence and all the quasi-evidence combine to show that Vergil was sexually timid in a way unprecedented for a functional Roman public figure; and this was *very* sexually timid. As noted before, the nickname Parthenias is a pun on *Vergilius/virgo*, *virgo* being the Latin translation *of parthenos,* a sheltered, unmarried girl. (The nickname may also refer to Vergil's Greek tutor Parthenius, though in his case it likely just connected him to the goddess Athena Parthenos as a protector; she was the patroness of Athens, the old capital of Greek literature.) Sexual abstinence in a man suggested oddity, not moral purity or religious commitment, as in the Christian era.

Roman sons of the well-to-do blew off considerable steam between a closely supervised adolescence and marriage some years later—not that marriage per se confined them, but the fuller responsibilities that came with it did take up time and impose some restraint and dignity. Before this, men sported convivially and lightheartedly, and few of their contacts afforded much privacy; in fact, commentary could circulate widely, as it did in the poems of Catullus.

I think the young "Verg-inal" was a terrified party-pooper and fell into the habit of staying away from the fun, perhaps with the excuse that the Muse was calling. His perfectionist hard work may have gotten an early assist from the need to have something to show for his absences that made the Muse's call appear genuine and worthwhile. He was, at any rate, popular, not an unpleasant recluse but someone to be drawn out and included whenever possible, someone whose inner life would not obtrude. The magical element in such a situation was misogyny; men did not respect erotic dependence on women and were apt to regard a companion who did not experience it as an elevated being, someone about whom to marvel, "He doesn't need women!" rather than about whom to suspect, "Does he need one of us?" Men took the sufficient delights of male friendship for granted.

But over time, one powerful patron's experience must have confirmed for Vergil the extent of the dangers for a man who evinced sexual nonconformity. Maecenas was in a position that must at first have seemed unassailable: he had vast wealth, he was the most able diplomat of his time, and Octavian in his rise and early rule trusted and relied on him. But Maecenas was not only exquisitely cultured and luxurious in his habits, he was also effeminate, with an appearance and mannerisms the Romans associated with alarming deviancy. Men without virility were supposed to lack all uprightness and moral fiber. Vergil harps on the theme of Eastern limpness in the *Aeneid:* an Italian warlord can even sneer at the Trojan refugees (progenitors of the Romans) as cowardly, daintily dressed, self-indulgent "Phry-gian women" (9.614–620). As I have already speculated, Vergil might have used his unrefined appearance and manner as a mask. Was it a deliberate contrast to the impression his patron gave?

A tightly interwoven problem was Maecenas' precious and af-fected literary style. At the safe distance of several decades after his death, Seneca the Younger devoted the whole of *Moral Letters* 114 to emphasizing the link between such a style and depravity, with Maecenas' work as the damning exhibit:

Maecenas' lifestyle is too well known to need any remarks on it here. We know how he walked, how swishy he was, and how he itched to show off; we also know how unwilling he was for his vices to be hidden. What, then? Doesn't the floppiness of his speaking style go right along with his flowing clothing? Are his habits, his entourage, his house, his wife any less blatant than his words? He could have been a man of great character had he pursued that goal down a straighter road, and not dodged comprehensible language, and not been as slack in speech as in his behavior. You will therefore see that his oratorical style was a drunk's: circling back, wandering off, and full of insolent disregard for the rules.

What is more shameful than these words: "A stream, its bank having long forest tresses"? And see how "they plow the channel with skiffs and, turning up the shallows, leave behind gardens." Or, "He gives a woman's grimace, puckers and bills and coos with his lips, and begins to sigh, like kings of silvan uplands who consecrate themselves with down-drooping necks." Or, "The incorrigible gang rummage through houses with viands and test them with a flagon and, using hope, exact death"; " . . . the tutelar god scarcely a witness to his own celebration"; or "a mother or wife beclothes the hearth with threads of flimsy wax and ground grain that crackles when burned." (4–5)

In Seneca's condemnation, "his wife" marks a scandal that may have been the occasion for Maecenas' relegation from the Augustan circle. Augustus reportedly had a liaison with Maecenas' wife, and the implication would have been plain: her husband could not service her. Dependent poets might not have forfeited Maecenas' financial support, or perhaps even his private friendship, but they had prided themselves on the public association with a man so powerful, clever, and affable, as well as generous. Horace addresses him affectionately in several poems, but the later *Epistles* 1.7 is an obnoxious palinode: Horace, staying much longer than promised on the farm that was Maecenas' gift, pleads not illness but the mere fear of illness, and the dullness and sluggishness of old age, and offers to return all that his patron has given him, if that is the price of his freedom. The letter feels like a companion piece for the sycophantic lyric poetry Horace wrote for Augustus around the same time and published in 17 BCE, a couple of years after Vergil's death. Historical sources do not give a date for the rift between Maecenas and Augustus, but there is no mention of the former in the *Aeneid*, after the resounding praises in the *Georgics*.

As to style, Vergil certainly was not as coy and fussy as Maecenas. (Without firm context, quotations like Seneca's can be rather baffling, and the translations above represent only my own gee-whiz efforts.) But Vergil resembles him to a degree unique among the major Augustan poets. First, both love personification; Vergil himself cites plant tresses at *Georgics* 4.137, after lines about winter frost shattering boulders and "reining in" rivers. Both authors sport rare, rather strained vocabulary. Vergil did not do this nearly as often as Maecenas apparently did, but he managed to provoke critics on these grounds, as I have shown. Both men use far-out, vivid, highly compressed expressions, especially concerning landscape: Vergil in *Aeneid* 6.724, at the start of a dizzyingly far-reaching description of how the divine essence infuses the universe, writes about the sea as "the flowing fields." Finally, both have a disconcerting tendency to place moralistic or traditional material in ornate, highly emotive language, even when style and subject matter, or details and theme, clash. Maecenas' submissive dove-y lover is rather sickening; the bird's neat beak is replaced with mobile lips, and the lowered head could be shorthand for giving oral sex, which a respectable man was supposed to receive only; but a real courting dove *is* doing the proper thing with every movement, so the comparison seems gratuitously perverse. Maecenas' noxious gang somehow uses food and drink for criminal predation on homes, but a feast with delicacies and large earthen vessels of wine was traditional, and this is time-honored vocabulary. Why *wouldn't* a *genius*, or tutelar god, witness or attest to his own rituals? The women are clearly performing immemorial rites — but the description is highly pretentious, and their candles are flimsy or slim or ductile; the Alexandrian-type image conveys exquisite — or over-refined — taste. Though his style is much better, Vergil constantly turns traditional language for traditional content inside out: instead of ordinary animal similes, he employs choreographic and melodramatic ones; he narrates feasts and sacrifices not with repetitious formulas but with something unusual expressed about every object and movement. Theocritus had greatly prettified poetry, Apollonius of Rhodes and Lucretius pushed the boundaries of epic. Vergil has no time for anything that gets in the way of vividness and emotion.

Of course Maecenas, far more than Vergil, was flying by the seat of his literary pants. Not only was his style much more extreme, but he used it in oratory; this is where Seneca's examples of verbal monstrosities appear to come from. Julius Caesar himself, a noted orator, had taken a didactic interest in style and written a treatise including prescriptions for a super-narrow native Latin vocabulary.

The treatise is extant only in fragments, but what it generally conveyed can be inferred from Caesar's prose in his war memoirs: bare-bones simplicity even at the cost of much repetition of words and forms. Maecenas blasted away at this principle by bringing into solemn civic arenas a wild elaboration and fantasy that many people would have sniffed at even in poetry. Long after Seneca, he was still inspiring satirical images of the orator as the opposite of what he should be: dressed swishily, gesturing insinuatingly – the would-be statesman was a secret *cinaedus* or fag.

All this suggests one reason Vergil avoided the public spotlight. If he composed far from Rome, visited the capital seldom, and released poems for other, much more powerful people to promote, dissociating his work from his person as much as possible, he could not be accused of undermining the lofty, highly serious role of a public man by the kind of man he was. That was Maecenas' great failing, according to Seneca.

The mere personal association and stylistic similarities were bad enough for Vergil's reputation. Suetonius writes, "Marcus Vipsanius called Vergil a substitute child of Maecenas, who was the founder of a new kind of bad derivative style, neither bombastic nor humble, but consisting of ordinary words and therefore sneaky" (Life 44). The critic quoted is Agrippa, a friend, general, and engineer-surveyor-architect of Augustus', who came from an obscure background but grew to be so important that he became the emperor's son-in-law and thus a co-founder of the Julio-Claudian dynasty. As a technical author himself but perhaps no more elaborately educated than Augustus, he may have taken a dim view of the more literary men in the inner circle, who far outnumbered him. The criticism reported here – if the wording is reliable – suggests a vicious and narrow-minded attack: Vergil fraudulently takes the place of the heir Maecenas cannot beget, and in literature Maecenas' (sometime?) choice of a middle way and common language was supposed to cover something defective. It sounds as if even Maecenas' less flamboyant literary style was being called merely closeted. Or the original text may have called *Vergil* dishonest for his lower-key style.

There is another way to translate the start of the smear, because the same verb denotes the physical subjugation of a person or animal, by "placing him under" a burden or in harness: "Marcus Vipsanius complained that [Vergil] was placed under the yoke by Maecenas . . ." Victors symbolically sent captive armies "under the yoke," and for individuals the yoke seems to have been an ancestor of the stocks or pillory: it bent the back down and kept the arms up, helpless: the buttocks stuck out, vulnerable. A man put down by the limp-wristed Maecenas was low indeed. Suetonius also mentions Carvilius the Painter's critique of the *Aeneid*, which was called "the *Aeneid*-whip" (Life 44). Whips were for slaves; the law exempted a Roman citizen from corporal punishment. The title may imply that the work's author is physically so degraded that he as well as his work is liable to whipping. But the obvious and perhaps the only reference here is literary: Zoilus of Amphipolis was nicknamed the "Homer-whip" for his fierce criticism of Homer.

Though Vergil probably left no direct communications about himself on the topic of eroticism and erotic love (the authenticity of the "Slight Poems" being a long shot), his wholly fictional works leave no doubt about his fear and pain. There are no grounds for speculating about specific experiences, but the unusual negativity of the sources he favors and of his narrative inventions place him in a special emotional category. Granted, the Romans in general were no fans of infatuation and the resulting loss of self-control, and their authors used a variety of distancing literary modes, such as attributing destructive passion to females particularly, limiting it to circumscribed tragic episodes, fencing it off emotionally with humor and contempt, and (a favorite) showing it to be effectively suppressed by civilizing violence. Vergil supercharges these modes, and also goes deeper. Here he is in a passage of *Eclogues* 8, in the voice of a pastoral singer, Damon:

> Inside our hedges, I saw you, a little girl
> With her mother, picking dewy apples (I was your leader).
> The year after the eleventh had just taken me in;
> From the ground I could now grasp the breakable branches.
> The instant I saw, I was done for, and a terrible folly stole me away.
>
> (37–41)

The lines (particularly the last) have such strong Theocritean influences as to suggest a collage, but their combination and the added details create a work of art such as the ancient world had not seen yet. Here in Vergil, the depiction of erotic obsession has risen above a joke but also sunk below tragedy; it does not have the timely quality necessary for either. It is, as in Proust, in every important sense permanent, a state built into the self; and as a statement about the human condition, it is an eternal dirge.

In Vergil, a young boy has had this experience; the speaker was and remains fundamentally unlike the grown-up Theocritean herdsmen courting aggressively within their own class, or the seduced and abandoned Theocritean girl who casts furious spells at her seducer but, apparently satisfied with the prospect of revenge, winds up with a gracious farewell to the moon and stars as dawn comes (*Idylls* 2). According to the ancient system of inclusive reckoning for units of time (which counts our zero unit as the first unit), the speaker here was thirteen, not twelve, when he fell in love; but the words of his reckoning at any rate sound childish, as if he vividly remembers not being used to the new, highly consequential year added to his age. He was the *dux* or "leader" (it can mean "general") to a mother and young daughter, both of them touchingly humanized in very few words, yet placed out of available erotic range by their ages and by their relationship to each other as protector and protected. The younger one is well below puberty, or "little"; near puberty she would be considered substantially grown up and marriageable or, if a slave, already available for sex. In ancient literature men ordinarily feel a fatherly tenderness at most for small girls, not desire or infatuation. The mother and daughter seem to need both permission to gather fruit (the scene takes place "inside our hedges/enclosures") and help in reaching it, and so depend on a boy who can barely reach it himself. The Latin verb for that action means "touch," "seize," and also "defile," and these branches, unlike the usual strong and pliant ones holding ripe fruit, are "breakable."

The scene suggests anguish in familiar romantic terms, which go back at least to Homer: the erotic appeal of the female dissolves male power to the point of disaster. But the location of the anguish so early in life, the vivid yet everyday details of its genesis, the impression of a secret told only now, in the maturity of despair, are all unusual. The agony starting from before the speaker could name it lasts forever. The voluble, even showily suicidal, Theocritean-type passions in the *Eclogues,* though the infusion of grief into the landscape is impressive, are rather ridiculous in comparison to what these few lines convey.

In the *Georgics,* the delights of the countryside at peace are set against the excesses of civil war, but purely natural erotic drives are condemned in parallel. The lust-crazed bulls, metaphoric warriors under the influence (described as a burning, wasting disease, as if from a witch's poison) of the femme fatale cow wound each other to no good purpose. The loser, a humiliated exile, trains until he can return and wreak revenge (3.215–241). But passion is dire for all species – and Vergil wanders into biological absurdity, showing a lioness forgetting her cubs and wandering "more savage" over the plains (245–246), instead of merely hunting more diligently in order to keep up her milk and bring them meat, and evincing no interest in mating again until they are able to survive on their own. Mares may totally lose the plot and when in heat seek not stallions but wilderness solitude and impregnation by the wind. In their retreat to remote stormy regions, they produce a substance called "horse-madness," which evil stepmothers use in baneful potions (266–283).

Orpheus' passion for his dead partner shows a similar overkill. He braves all the perils of the underworld to retrieve her, armed only with his music, and he cannot bear to have her following him unseen until they reach the upper world: he turns to look at her and loses her a second, more excruciating time. Disabled except for tuneful, lonely mourning, he is set on by the ultimate maddened females, the Bacchantes, who are jealous of his devotion and send his severed head, still calling Eurydice's name, floating down a river. Talk about undying love.

Toward the far end of Vergil's creative arc is the *Aeneid*'s Andromache, a fellow Trojan survivor whom Aeneas finds unconsoled by her restored freedom, a new realm that imitates Troy, and a second Trojan husband who has now escaped slavery himself to become its king. Her sufferings remain foremost in her mind:

> By chance Andromache was in the woods
> Beside the river "Simoïs," offering
> The ritual food and gifts to Hector's ashes,
> To call his spirit at the hollow green mound

And the two altars sacred to her tears.

She saw me coming in my Trojan armor

And froze, beside herself, stunned by the portent.

As she stood gazing, all warmth left her body.

She fainted. Finally, she could speak, and said,

"Goddess' son, is it you I see—alive?

You're really here—with news? But if you've lost

The kind light, where is Hector?" Now her tears gushed,

Her wailing filled that place; I was distressed,

And as she raved, I struggled with a few words:

"I am alive, through all of my ordeals.

Don't doubt your eyes.

Andromache, you were the wife of Hector.

How far you fell! But has some worthy fate

Now caught you? Or is Pyrrhus still your husband?"

She bent her head and whispered this to me:

"Lucky beyond us all was Priam's daughter,

Compelled to die beside a hostile grave

Beneath Troy's high walls. No lots drawn for her,

No conqueror's bed to take her prisoner!

Hauled past remote seas once my homeland burned,

I bore the insults of Achilles' son.

I had a child in slavery. Pyrrhus, chasing

A Spartan bride, Hermione, Leda's grandchild,

Gave me to Helenus, another slave."

(3.301–329)

Homer acknowledges the sexual slavery that women on the losing side of warfare suffered, but he does not dwell on it. Athenian tragedy (*Agamemnon*, *The Trojan Women*) does dwell on it, but within certain boundaries, chiefly those of formal lament and violent comeuppance. Vergil insists that Andromache's erotic humiliations are, like her bereavements, without boundaries. For her, as for the reminiscent Damon in *Eclogues* 8, and for Orpheus, this is life now, a container for grief.

Dido and Aeneas' shameful union betrays both their nations. Cupid's poison induces her love frenzy, and the couple first have sex in a dark cave during a violent storm, with nymphs shrieking in the background. The affair's start—where we would expect hope and tenderness—is more like a horror movie than a typical literary romance. "From this day came catastrophe and death," the poet announces (4.169). Aeneas leaves Dido by Jupiter's decree, having taken her on through Venus his mother's mischief, and the parting escalates from excruciations of rage, humiliation, manipulation, and griefs both present and many years old to actual danger to all the Trojans and catastrophe for Dido and her Phoenicians. Aeneas hurries to escape with his countrymen—first hiding the work of loading and rigging the fleet—because he fears a violent attack, an idea with which she does toy. She is terrified that her earlier, rejected suitors will close in, and the fire from her giant pyre of self-immolation does their work for them; though far out at sea, the departing Trojans can see the flames that throw the city into chaos. But even this scene is not conclusive: her agony will continue in the underworld, where she will project it onto the still living Aeneas.

In many other instances in the *Aeneid* (Vergil's only undoubted work of sustained narration) a woman's allure or her own desire proves disastrous: when Aeolus accepts the bribe of a voluptuous young nymph and almost destroys the Trojans along with their ships (the waves reaching heaven and baring strips of the sea floor); when Helen has her second Trojan husband, Deiphobus, killed and mutilated in their bed; when Amata is creepily, clingily obsessed with obtaining Turnus as a son-in-law, no matter what the cost in lives; when the mere sight — as in the *Eclogues,* that is all it takes — of the demure Lavinia now red-faced and sobbing in the center of this debacle inflames Turnus to fight to the end for her even if he destroys their shared world in the process.

The nymph Juturna's agony, like Dido's, actually lasts beyond mortal life. Raped by Jupiter and then compensated with deification (she is a female Ganymede), she is not allowed to keep using her supernatural powers on the battlefield to save her brother Turnus but is driven away and forced to desert him:

> At last I'll leave the field. No need to threaten,
> Hideous birds. I know your deadly wingbeats;
> I know the will of Jupiter, high-minded,
> High-handed. But can this be how he pays
> For my virginity? He made me deathless,
> And yet if I could die, I'd end my anguish
> And go with my poor brother through the shadows.
> What is the good of my unending life
> Without you? Can the earth gape wide enough
> To drop me to the shades, though I'm immortal?
>
> (12.875–884)

Though all these characters' suffering might on a shallow view seem quintessentially heterosexual, an author who knows what he is doing, like Proust, can substitute female for male without a hitch in an account of desire and obsession. But also like Proust, when Vergil eventually comes to write originally about erotic love between males (in the *Eclogues* this topic derives heavily from Theocritus), it is not in a lighthearted way; he does not come across as comfortable with his sexuality and liable to reject only opposite-sex relationships as grim and futureless.

His great tale of two male lovers, Nisus and Euryalus, does not rise to tragedy because it contains no plausible hope and therefore creates little suspense and no crucial moral conflict: these are simply two people being their inexorably doomed selves. But there *is* twin hubris, the self-destruction of two appealing characters on the same side through their egotistical folly. Nisus is older, and should be the leader and protector, but his impulsiveness has caused him to cheat openly in order to throw the footrace to his lover Euryalus in 5.317–338. In book 9, Nisus decides on the spy mission out of a restless urge for glory, and he lets the equally impetuous Euryalus come with him in spite of his own initial scruples. He takes the lead in slaughtering sleeping enemies, which wastes vital time. He lets Euryalus keep a gleaming looted helmet on his head to betray him to a hostile band of hardened warriors. He loses Euryalus behind him as the two flee through a woodland, and he returns for a showy, suicidal rescue attempt.

The story gives a realistic sense of young people getting in over their heads together. This is, after all, a first love affair for a couple who have almost no family at hand to advise and look after them, which was probably Vergil's own case in his teens and early twenties; it was probably also the case for most of his peers in a time of military and political upheaval, when male elders had more urgent things to think about than their sons and grandsons.

It might seem logical for fantasy to come into the story of the two young male lovers. Would not Vergil have dreamed of a love affair working out for himself, and lasting, and would he not have applied this dream, in some form, to his epic masterpiece? Why is there no happily-ever-after ending for Nisus and Euryalus? As it is, the only thing saved is their story, through the power of Vergil's poetry (9.446–449).

My answer is that there were some things even Vergil's imagination could not manage. Roman society — much less that society's most authoritative poem — had no room for two men, who belonged to each other to the permanent exclusion of others, growing old together in their own household; fellow Romans would have nipped even the fantasy in the bud. In myth, a virtuous married couple such as Philemon and Baucis or Deucalion and Pyrrha can be saved through supernatural protection and look toward a happy old age and a death at the same time, because their relationship is the pattern of home and true love that pushed out other potential patterns. The best thing Vergil could do with Nisus and Euryalus was kill them off young and gloriously and not think of them growing older and being separated.

This kind of hopelessness would naturally lead to a build-up of rage. In the *Aeneid,* the famous *furor* or uncontrollable frenzy that an Amata or a Turnus undergoes comes from a longing for an object that is literally within reach but utterly unobtainable, and it shoots its victim outdoors and into public exposure as insane. Amata may fondle and dote on Turnus — she must have him and no one else as a son-in-law — but getting her way would leave him even more forbidden to her. Poisoned with the Fury Allecto's venom, she runs alone through the city, on display as a madwoman (7.376–384). Turnus himself, in looking at the beautiful, weeping Lavinia, the prize in a conflict he is fated to lose, hurls himself, incandescent with fury, out of the palace to prepare for the fight that will destroy him. The sparks fly from his face; he is like a bull charging against a tree trunk (12.64–106). To show desire is to be physically exposed to the world as possessed by it, and the logical end of the possession is death. Better to be an Aeneas: glum, dutiful, receding from all human attachments, especially those of the body.

Again, literary tradition presides; it virtually decrees what the author can communicate about the world and himself. The fury of love was a long-standing theme in literature we know Vergil and his circle read. Catullus 64, in which Ariadne stands on the shore of Naxos, wild with grief and rage over her lover Theseus' clandestine departure, obviously helped inspire the depiction of Dido's reaction to her own abandonment.

But, also again, I want to stress selectivity. The erotic running amok that Euripides, Apollonius of Rhodes, Catullus, and Vergil all depict does not represent a purely scholarly imitation in the later authors; like all other borrowings, it involves choice, and choice implicates lived experience. Euripides himself, on the evidence of Aristophanes, was considered a misogynist outlier in his own time, and the other great tragedians do appear more balanced; they all chose and shaped their material to suit themselves as well as their public. The later vogue for Euripides' work, and the tendency to imitate it, may have found special support in an Alexandrian literary establishment that operated like an all-male university, with a common dining hall and other facilities meant to absorb most of its members' time and attention – not a place presumably friendly to flights of romantic passion. Nevertheless, Callimachus left stories ("Berenike's Lock of Hair," "Acontius and Cydippe") bursting with the adorability of powerful but mainstream and sanctioned eroticism. Why did such works not furnish *the* story from then on? The influential Catullus' life – a powerful, reckless, and scandal-ridden adulteress made a fool of him – could help explain why the Euripidean and not the Callimachean strain prevailed to become dominant in Augustan Rome. But even Catullus depicts believable delights of his relationship. And even Euripides left the happily-ever-after *Alcestis:* in that case, hugely unlike that of the *Georgics'* Orpheus and Eurydice, a husband gets his wife back after her death; she died in the first place out of self-sacrificing conjugal love. Vergil's demonstrations that erotic desire and romantic attachment are dangerous and futureless remain unabating throughout the work he undoubtedly wrote.

But there is something else striking about the relationship between Vergil's eroticism and his work. His early experiences, whatever they were, and however hopeful or bad they were, did not notably wear out his passion as a writer. Nothing is more usual in writers than such a late-life decline, depressingly reified in their output if they do continue to write out of habit or for money or affirmation. W. B. Yeats was an exception, striking in preserving his creative energy long past his youth (in spite of a long, obsessive infatuation that embittered him), so that much of his best work came later. He managed, in a way that appears miraculous, to keep at a self-punishing grind of revision, yet he maintained, even intensified, his imaginative excitement once it was separate from the world of youth that pours its spirit away in coupling. He described his later mood, a longing for the eternity of art, in the poem "Sailing to Byzantium."

Another example of course is Proust, a prisoner by choice of his soundproofed room for the later years of his life, reconstructing erotic obsession in enormous sentences mimicking coitus that refuses to end. Yet another example is Milton. He held out for a beautiful young girl he imagined would be tender, biddable, and supportively studious — the perfect solution to his perfectionist loneliness, as well as a perfect erotic outlet. Soon his bride left him, and he began a much-ridiculed campaign to liberalize English divorce law in order to be completely rid of her and marry again; so distressed and humiliated was he by his situation, and so desperate for domestic and erotic companionship, that his opinions about marriage seem actually to have extended to condoning polygamy, which would have allowed him to dispense with a divorce and marry a woman he was then pursuing. After three years, his wife returned, probably because of a political reversal that had thrown her family into poverty. She died giving birth to their fourth child. A second wife also died in childbirth; a third marriage, to a much younger woman, was reportedly very happy. But probably nothing could have been as satisfying as his relationship with his Muse, Urania or the Sky Woman, who came to him every night with a long passage of *Paradise Lost;* the blind poet needed only to dictate it to an assistant in the morning. Urania was the prelapsarian Eve, there for *him,* just as he was, and with no needs of her own.

What *about* the far-fetched dei ex machina in the *Aeneid?* Literary critics sniff at them because they plunk down from Olympus or elsewhere whenever the hero needs them: for help and comfort, for instructions, for a prod onward, for intervention at the needful moment, for magic weaponry to save his life and win him a homeland. Supernatural signs also revive the hero at times of doubt, danger, and stagnation. But if the theme of divine intervention is taken biographically and related to poetic inspiration and the poetic calling as superior substitutes for ordinary eroticism, then it has a coherent symbolism of great persuasiveness. Typically, the visitations are at night, bringing a release from tension and an assurance of personal continuity. Here are the Penates, or home gods, appearing to Aeneas in *Aeneid* 3:

> Night had brought sleep to all who live on earth.
> The sacred forms of Trojan household gods
> That I had rescued from the city's flames
> Appeared before my eyes as I was lying
> Asleep. They stood out plainly in the bright light
> The moon was pouring through my open window.

Love and Art

They seemed to speak to me and soothe my worry.
"What the god would have told you at his shrine,
He kindly sends by us, right to your threshold.
When Troy was burned, we soldiered after you.
We crossed the swelling water with your fleet,
And we will raise your children to the stars
And give the wide earth to your city. High walls
For your high gods you'll need there. Do not shirk
Hard travel to a new home, since Apollo
Did not intend your settling here in Crete.
There is a place Greeks call Hesperia,
An old land, strong in war and rich in loam.
Oenotrians lived there, whose descendants take
Their name, it's said, from Italus the king.
This is our own home."

(3.147–167)

Once Vergil went inward with his desires and his quest for fulfilment, the beloved that was his own imagination proved more faithful to him, and brought him more satisfaction, than any lover could have. As Aeneas accepts the divine armor with power, beauty, order, and meaning built in, Vergil could accept the gift of his own artistry.

Snowy-white holy Venus brought her presents
Through heaven's clouds. Far off, she saw her son
In a secluded valley, by a cold stream.
She went straight up to him and spoke these words:
"My husband's gifts are finished, with the skill
He pledged. So don't hang back from challenging
The arrogant Laurentians or fierce Turnus."

Then the Cytherean embraced her son,
And set the gleaming arms beneath the oak.
The goddess' gift – the honor of it – thrilled him.
He couldn't fill his gaze with every piece.
With awe he picked them up and turned them over:
The fearsome helmet with its flaming crest,
The deadly sword, the blood-red corselet stiff
With bronze – enormous, like a cloud, blue-shaded
But kindling with the sky's far-stretching rays;
Then the smooth greaves of forged gold and electrum,
The spear, the shield – work beyond all description.
There the fire god had etched Italian history
And Roman triumphs, from the prophecies
He knew: Ascanius' whole line to come,
And every war the clan would fight, in sequence.

(8.608–629)

The moment the hero accepts his gift is the moment when the fear of failure falls away, as it never quite can in a relationship with another person. The artist who has made peace with his talent makes peace with the future.

And there is not only peace but joy, the transports of a voyage to Byzantium, as it were, that the mind can invoke at will. In *Aeneid* 4, the Trojans hate being stuck in Carthage, held back from their destined country while Aeneas pursues a pointless and self-indulgent affair. Aeneas himself, it turns out, can hardly get away fast enough, starting secret preparations in response to the first divine command, and the "love" that makes him wretched when confronting Dido sounds more like guilt and embarrassment. He sets sail with alacrity, his crews cheering, toward the place out of which Vergil creates so many further mesmerizing vistas. In strict didactic terms, Italy is the place of lofty purpose, and rest, and sustenance. But poetically it is a bright quilt of rivers and plains and uplands and glens seen more vividly, loved more intensely, than ever before in literature. It is the visionary country.

> Greased fir slid through the shallows; woods and water
> Wondered to see strange things: the warriors' shields
> Shining far off, and painted, swimming hulls.
> The men wore out a day and night in rowing
> Up the long bends. Trees of all kinds gave shelter,
> And the keels cut the virid, still reflections.

(8.91–96)

CHAPTER SIX

The Work Takes Over

Though little is known about how Vergil spent his days, one indirect piece of evidence is the extremely slow rate of production for his second and third major works. For the *Georgics,* the average rate was around a line a day; for the *Aeneid,* around two lines, if we rely on the seven- and twelve-year composition periods, respectively, that Suetonius cites (Life 25): these comport with the historical context and the other information about Vergil's life. The *Eclogues* may have materialized at a similar rate, but since pieces might date from his apprentice period, I would not try to calculate the speed of its composition as a whole, based on the three-year period named in the same passage of the biography.

As in their innate struggles with language itself, Vergil and Octavian were eerily similar in their slow and dogged progress toward their lives' main goals — allowing of course for the great differences between literary excellence and unchallenged power. Even a certain synchrony is evident, reflecting their collaborative purposes. Vergil may have started the final stage of the *Eclogues'* composition, if not the poem itself, late in 42, the year of the Battle of Philippi that placed Octavian, Lepidus, and Antony in effective control of Roman domains. *Eclogues* 1 celebrates Octavian as a godlike and providential leader, able to mitigate the suffering and upheaval of civil war caused by land confiscations after a major victory of his — these probably would be events of 41. *Eclogues* 4 seems to celebrate the Treaty of Brundisium of the year 40, ceding Antony the eastern realms and solidifying the arrangement with a marriage between him and Octavian's sister. But the ten poems were apparently not finished until the year 39 or 38.

In the *Georgics* Vergil imagines conducting a Triumph for Octavian (3.10–39) and includes other zealous commendations of the man. The *Georgics* was likely completed in 30 and the *Aeneid* started not long afterward; 31 was the year the Battle of Actium, and after clean-up operations Octavian achieved a species of sole rule, though he was to maintain many republican structures of power sharing and consultation. He assumed the name Augustus in the year 27. A rough pattern thus appears of Vergil producing and promising suitable works around the times of great transitions in Octavian's earlier career.

But in the production of the *Aeneid,* a work that was to broadcast Augustus' ambitions — eternal world dominion for Rome, the establishment of a dynasty worshipped alongside the Olympian gods — Augustus must have confronted the same fact that dogged his governance: in spite of what consolidated power seemed to promise, it was even harder to get what he wanted in (relative) peacetime than it had been to smash substantial opposition through all-out war. He did not, for example, gain full control of the Senate until the year of Vergil's death, 19 BCE. The actual — and grinding, and on occasion disastrous — push to expand the borders far into areas of Europe where Rome had had little or no presence began only in

16 BCE. Administrative reforms, transformative legislation, monuments, public works, and crushed rebellions continued to fall slowly into place until Augustus' death in 14 CE.

Hence Octavian's impatience for the completed *Aeneid* is understandable. Vergil's colleague the love elegist Propertius was allowed, or instructed, to rejoice in a poem that "something greater than the *Iliad* is being born" (quoted in Suetonius, *Life* 30), to which both Roman and Greek authors were commanded to give way — as if the swaddled prince of an epic would soon be on display. (Reproduction was, maybe not incidentally, a source of a major frustration for Augustus. He had no son of his own to succeed him, and arranged marriages that should have oversupplied him with heirs, but the death of his nephew Marcellus in early adulthood — he is lamented in *Aeneid* 6.860–886 — was only the most devastating of his disappointments.) That this poem, line for line, came together around twice as fast as the *Georgics* is a sign of relative haste. The poet probably had increased material and social incentives. We see in Suetonius (*Life* 31) that Augustus wheedled and humorously threatened in order to hear several books of the *Aeneid* recited; the emperor no doubt felt that recitation formalized completion and was trying to pressure the poet like an ordinary contractor.

But Vergil was absorbed in a task far bigger (twelve books, after the *Georgics'* four) and more complicated (dozens of characters and episodes, a great variety of detailed settings and other descriptions). Signs of dead ends never resolved remain in the half-lines scattered throughout the poem: Vergil planned to return to them later; he had long been skipping around in order to spread the tensions of his perfectionism more evenly — which was not, apparently, a method that filled the management with glee. Modern publishers would recognize the problem: it is not the more usual one of making an author work but instead of prying a manuscript, long finished to an acceptable standard, from his viselike grip.

It was not that Vergil failed to have his own version of a good time. Though fame aggravated the poet's physical shyness, when it came to his actual work, he could be surprisingly open and interactive, and even something of a show-off. His proud inventiveness extended to his methodologies (if that is not too stern a term for some quite free and instinctive proceedings). Here is Suetonius:

> While he was writing the *Georgics*, it is reported, he dictated by habit each day a large number of verses he had composed in the morning, and spent the rest of the day reducing them to a very small number — he cleverly remarked about this that he formed his poem the way a she-bear forms her cub, by licking it into shape little by little. When it came to the *Aeneid*, he first wrote a draft in prose, then divided it into twelve books, and then began to transform it piece by piece into verse, laying hold of the different parts in whatever order he pleased. And to keep the thrust of his activity unbroken, he left certain things unfinished, and (so to speak) propped other things up with provisional words. He used to say jokingly that these were put in like struts, to support the structure until the sturdy columns arrived. . . .
>
> He gave readings to somewhat larger audiences as well, but not often, and usually of passages he was unsure about, so that he could test what people thought of them. They say that during his extreme old age Eros, his freedman assistant, used to tell about Vergil once finishing two half-verses on the spot in the course of a reading. He had only the words "Misenus, son of Aeolus" in one line, and he added "who had no rival"; in the next line was "In summoning men with a bronze horn," and he added to it "and rousing Mars with music," which was tossed off with a similar headiness, and he instantly ordered Eros to add both half-lines to the scroll. (Life 22–34)

For the *Georgics'* very slow composition, the "licking," simply in terms of going over a passage again and again, relentlessly, is plausible. So is the outlining and filling-in work on the *Aeneid;* so is the historicity of these consultation sessions, occasions too strange to invent. Authors of the time liked to project ease and mastery, not that they were groping. But the sessions could not have brought many useful reactions; no one Vergil knew except Horace would have been expert enough to advise him well. But it is easy to intuit other purposes. Merely reading a draft to others would have given Vergil a fresh feel for it and allowed him to better imagine a stage at which he would be ready to let it go.

I wonder about the reported slam-dunk completion of a pair of *Aeneid* lines during a reading. The source—his own assistant— sounds good, but what was he getting at with the anecdote? That Vergil could usually, or only rarely (his rate of progress points to this), see an instant solution to a two-part problem? That it showed characteristic, or uncharacteristic, self-possession for him to be able to think on his feet this way? In any event, this is not how a straight-forward aptitude works. Horace, who moved between meters and genres with gymnastic skill, must have pulled similar stunts all the time in the privacy of his study.

This was an era when facility in composition was greatly valued— though Horace does sneer at it as a supreme value, citing the primitive satirist Lucilius, who could burble out hundreds of lines "while standing on one foot" (*Satires* 1.4.9–10). The Alexandrians, the Neoterics, and now the Augustans had in fact all been involved in pulling literature out of the arena of spectator sports and making it more refined, through scholarship and exquisite craftmanship.

Hence if there is one thing that a just consideration of Vergil's life requires, it is a look at time. How did Vergil get enough of it, from a regime that was stingy only with this, and from a society that was not used to conceding it to the individual in the first place? How did he secure entire mornings for poetic outpouring, and entire afternoons for ruthless and thorough revision?

Perhaps he was even fitting in more than one literary project at a time. It is possible that while he worked on the books we know, Vergil had other drafts in progress, which could have fallen away or gone into storage to await revision, some eventually figuring in the *Appendix Vergiliana*. Illness, rest, travel, or administration of his finances or entourage (though the degree of his involvement in any kind of administration was probably a choice) could also interrupt his work for certain periods. And what about that inexorable and most constant demand, Roman sociability? Friendships clearly did him a great deal of good, both emotional and professional, in his youth. But the payback, the attention and credit his promoters and supporters expected as he emerged to do great things, would have been an acute irritation and a wearing distraction. If the number of names and the amount of flattery in the *Eclogues* as opposed to the *Aeneid* is any sign, he cut back on his social life — or at least his publicly accountable social life — ruthlessly in the interim.

He had to. The refinement of his verses testifies to sustained concentration away from the spotlight. One of Vergil's most famous lines is the recasting of cartoonish words reflecting court poetry of the Alexandrian Callimachus. In Callimachus' book of origin stories (surviving only in fragments) called the *Aetia* (Causes) is the tale of "Berenike's Lock of Hair," which usually goes by the Latin title "Coma Berenices." The Greek poem celebrated a Ptolemaic dynastic marriage and was imitated by Catullus; the sickly, un-Catullan mannerisms of the result testify that it was more like a translation than an adaptation. "Unwilling, O queen, I withdrew from the top of your head" goes one line of the Latin poem (66.39). The hank of hair, a votive offering for the new husband's safety in the war he leaves the marriage bed to fight, is speaking. Vergil builds on Catullus, in whose Latin the line is "invita, o regina, tuo de vertice cessi." In the *Aeneid*, this becomes "invitus, regina, tuo de litore cessi," "Unwilling, queen, I withdrew from your shore," words Aeneas addresses to Dido's ghost in the underworld (6.460).

The newer line is thoroughly apt for Aeneas' particular kind of breast-beating. Some while earlier he extricated himself from his lover according to the divine command, a move that her hysteria and his and his followers' longing for their destined country made more desirable; she and her fate hardly preoccupied him thereafter. But now the sight of her angry ghost mortifies him. He responds with such fervent and self-centered redesign of reality that the question once flashed through my head, Are the gods themselves and their mission for him meant to seem a product of his imagination? Here is my English version of the passage.

> He wept and spoke to her in tender love:
> "Poor Dido, then the messenger was right—
> Your own hand held the blade that brought your death?
> And it was my fault? By the stars, the high gods,
> And any truth below the earth: my queen,
> It was against my will I left your country,
> And by the orders of the gods, who now
> Ordain my journey through this shadowed squalor,
> These depths of night. I couldn't have believed
> That I would bring such pain by my departure."
>
> (455–464)

The speech is a masterpiece of mendacity from an author who knew of what he wrote; he was, after all, a lover of males who composed the ancient world's most searing heterosexual love stories, those of Orpheus and Eurydice and of Dido and Aeneas. As the culmination of the passage, line 460 is a fittingly refashioned artifice. In Catullus, the lock of hair that speaks is grammatically feminine; it claims to be an admirer of the ruler's wife (technically a lesbian admirer, I guess), although it is a product of her own body: a more intense symbiotic sycophancy is hard to imagine. The lock's vaunted devotion as coiffure and its grief under the shears are risible, its apotheosis as a constellation baroque. The pretentious *o* of officious address in particular makes this bundle of dead cells sound like a flattering courtier. The *o* in this meter, adding a syllable, necessitates an elision, the dropping of another, unobtrusive syllable. Hence the feminine ending *-a* at the end of the first word in the line, *invita* (unwilling), is silent, and this makes the *o* even louder (so to speak) by contrast.

In Vergil's line, the speaker is forthrightly and confidently a man. This poet leaves out the *o*, creating a more intimate and natural-sounding tone and making room for the full *-us* masculine ending on the adjective: *invitus* is a masculine "unwilling." That *-us* at the start of the second metrical foot is functionally a long syllable, in contrast to the short feminine *-a* in the next word, *regina*, "queen." The forms speak: You may be a queen, and I am just a man, but because I am a man my will takes precedence even while I claim that it is not mine; the gods had no long-term plans for you, a widowed, childless woman in permanent exile, but I am the founder of the world's most important dynasty. By substituting "shore" (*litore*) for the expected "side" (*latere*) the speaker describes his departure from his lover in terms of geography rather than personal detachment, and this fits the broad context: if he had what he *wanted,* he protests in book 4, he would still be in Troy, tending the graves of loved ones and rebuilding the city (340–344); he did not part from Dido's *side* because he was never really there. There has been no true comity in their relationship, merely an exchange of humiliations, as the gracious, lavish rescuer of the desperate refugee became the emotionally enslaved, overindulgent lover, and then the sacrifice to his all-important mission. And despite all Aeneas' protests here in book 6 and back in book 4, his real desires show up even in the meter of line 6.460: the first part of the line comprises five long syllables, and what is left contains five long and four short ones — that is, all the short ones there are. Quantity and not stress (as in English meter) shapes the variable hexameter and determines how fast a line goes at different points. In this line, it is as if the speaker is first ploddingly addressing his former lover, then recalling how he skidded away from her. The surface of Vergil's story may invite us to take factitious assertions seriously, but the form, down to the smallest nuance, tends to undercut them, so that both the harmonies and the psychology are richer than English versions can show.

This kind of complex beauty is enthralling, and the meanings to which it can open the mind are virtually unlimited. Speaking only of allusion and adaptation (among many elements of composition), 6.460 subtly and precisely characterizes Aeneas as shallow and cynical. And Catullus and Callimachus do not inspire the only allusive and adaptative effects along these lines. Odysseus' meeting with Ajax's ghost in the underworld in *Odyssey* 11.543–564 plays a role too: there the durable, glib hero professes that he would rather not have won the contest for the dead Achilles' arms and armor, since Ajax went mad from the humiliation of his defeat and committed suicide; Odysseus wants justification on top of victory and invites Ajax to join him in blaming the will of Zeus. But Ajax, like

Dido, withdraws in enraged silence. Lovers as fighters and natural rivals in a world not big enough for the two of them; a discreditable winner and survivor who cannot let matters rest and demands the appearance of righteousness too; punishing destiny ruling over both of them; and an utter lack of final answers, even given nobility of purpose in life as long as it lasts—Vergil can culminate all this and more in a line like *Aeneid* 6.460.

This line is not even a particular high point of Vergil's craft, as I know from my work as his translator. Its odd provenance and its centrality to the hero's pleas in the authoritatively favored book 6 of the *Aeneid* and in reference to the blockbuster book 4 has brought it a lot of attention, but Vergil appears to have sweated as much over the brief speeches of walk-on characters never to be heard from again, over the description of passing landscapes, and over just about everything else.

His achievement is not the flow of relative facility but the hard-edged and gripping result of merciless work. In the natural iambic pentameter of English, I might struggle for a whole afternoon to form a line a quarter as impressive as its original—aware as I did that the hexameter is not a meter native to Latin and even excludes some important Latin words altogether, as their shapes can fit in nowhere. To compose in iambic pentameter is child's play by contrast. I felt myself in the presence of something more significant than supreme talent: it was some unknowable amount of talent united with a titanium will. As far as I'm concerned, Vergil damn well did compose the *Aeneid* at the average rate of two lines a day, and yes, he prodded and shaped in his own good time; no wonder incomplete lines remained at the time of his death.

The advances thus made over his closest predecessor in epic poetry, Lucretius, are phenomenal. Lucretius can fudge in order to cram a line full or stretch it out, as if it did not matter to him decisively which syllables were long or short. Vergil's hexameter is technically exquisite. More than that, each line is an adventure, without plug-in epic formulas or lazy repetitions of appealing inventions. Vergil treated the problems in his medium as opportunities for dramatic expression. Lucretius achieves some poetic high points, but he mainly plonks through scientific claims and predictable philosophical exhortations, like a piano student picking out a minuet a grade or two above her skill. Vergil meets the recalcitrant Latin hexameter head-on, beats it into submission, and puts it to work, creating subtle moods and characterizations, outlining scenes, and enhancing arguments.

The melding of form and content in Vergil is like the musical scene setting and storytelling of Beethoven, giving the impression of portentous depth and sympathy; the composition not only sounds good, it seems fused into fate and nature because the composer's ideas are so thoroughly fused into what are ordinarily mere formal elements: time, tone, pitch, shape.

I wrote in Chapter 1 about the striking angles from which landscape is seen in Vergil, and the dynamism of nature as a set of characters, probably in part as an influence of the author's childhood. But in his most masterful passages, especially in the *Aeneid*, human and animal and divine, tragically limited and gloriously omniscient points of view combine; even inanimate objects are endowed with thought and feeling and evoke deep sympathy, as in *Aeneid* 10.215–257:

Day had retreated from the sky. Kind Phoebe

Drove her night horses tramping through high heaven.

Aeneas (wakeful in anxiety)

Trimmed the sails or sat, steering, at the tiller.

Suddenly in midcourse a band of comrades

Appeared; the ships that kindly Cybele
Had changed to nymphs, goddesses of the sea —
One for each bronze beak that had stood on shore.
They swam along with him and sliced the waves.
Far off, they'd known their king; they danced around him.
Cymodocea, the most eloquent,
Came up behind, her right hand on the stern,
Her left hand softly paddling, breasts emerging.
He didn't know her. "Child of gods, Aeneas,
Are you awake? Then let the sails' rope go.
We are your fleet, pines from the holy heights
Of Ida — sea nymphs now. With sword and flame
The treacherous Rutulian hounded us.
We had to break your chains and seek you here.
The Mother pitied us, transformed us, sent us
To live a blessed life beneath the water.
The walls and moat imprison your young son
Among fierce Latins and their bristling spears.
Arcadian horsemen hold their posts, brave Tuscans
Along with them. But Turnus with his squadrons
Blocks them, resolved to keep your camps apart.
Rise up! Call your confederates to arms
At first dawn. Take the shield the god of fire
Has ringed with gold and made invincible.
Tomorrow's light — if you will trust my words —
Will see great heaps of the Rutulian dead."
She spoke and dove away, but first pushed deftly
At the high hull, which ran on through the waves
More swiftly than a spear or wind-quick arrow,
And the rest sped behind. Anchises' son,
The Trojan, stunned, then joyful, turned his gaze

To the sky's arch and prayed, "Idaean Mother
Of gods, devoted to Mount Dindymus,
Tower-crowned towns, and chariot-yoked lions:
Lead me in war, achieve your prophecy,
March with the Phrygians, bringing them good fortune."
The day, in its swift circle, had returned;
The ripe sun routed nighttime as he spoke.

The universe, in all its variety, is moving as one, and rolling in the single direction of fated events.

But what *was* Vergil's typical day? Is there any way to look beyond the conditions of patronage (both the typical ones and those in his individual case) and the public view of the composition and revision activities that produced such impressive results and see him actually living with his work? Probably not, but one thing seems clear: the scope for authors to shape their lifestyle was greater by the time he finished pushing against the edges.

It is a significant understatement that the authors who are read and taught the most transform books. They also transform the culture more generally, and they may do this not only through the contents of their books but also through the writing of their books. If they meet a world that is not geared for what they seek to do, they try to change it, and what they achieve for their own sakes — and even what they botch — can play out over time in surprisingly consequential ways.

Take the issue of a writer's day-to-day availability. Few people today raise an eyebrow when an aspiring writer (or at least one without pressing responsibilities at home) packs a van for a journey of self-discovery or moves into a cabin in the mountains. But such acceptance is not immemorial. It had to be won piece by piece, and paid for by work of extraordinary quality by a different kind of writer from the virtual public servant or the man with independent means and an avocation. Vergil captured more ground for a writing life than anyone else in pagan antiquity. It may be useful, then, to look at the conditions into which he arrived, and how little time, space, and privacy they allowed even privileged writers. We can see very little of how he negotiated his way through these constraints, but we can see the constraints.

The closest general analogy for ancient literary projects may be (sometimes literally) concrete public works. The state or its wealthy benefactors procured Athenian drama, Roman comedy, hymns such as Horace's "Song of the Ages," and other works for performance on specific public occasions to build up a regime's power and prestige and support the society's important functions. Forensic and political oratory addressed disputes and policy questions in the public arena. Even many works without any official status, such as Lucilius' satires, did public service as school texts, helping train the young in civic values. Schoolroom use is a fate Horace ironically expects for his own poems (*Epistles* 1.20.17–18), and it was an inevitable future of Vergil's. In a sense, especially since he worked under the head of the Roman Empire, Vergil was one more contractor, like a tax collector or a harbor dredger. But as we have seen, with the *Aeneid* at least, the contractor did not deliver promptly, and the emperor complained. Vergil, however, needed latitude, and he claimed it in part by avoiding a fixed domicile. Augustus would no doubt have preferred him to live near himself, in the fast lane that was Rome. But Vergil apparently never settled anywhere.

A home took an inordinate amount of time and attention. An upper-class Roman citizen fed his self-importance on not having an hour to himself. Where there was no family to distract him, he still dictated letters, received petitioners, and deliberated over decisions too important for his manager(s) to make. His time spent in bathing, dining, exercise, and connoisseurship was intensely social; he was on display and interacting with others almost all day and all evening. He might well nod off at night on a convivial couch and not turn in to his bedroom or start back toward his own home until near dawn.

A scholar like the polymath Pliny the Elder might seem an exception; Pliny the Younger describes in his published *Letters* (3.5) the basis of his uncle's prolific output: how, for example, he worked during sunbaths and on the road in his vehicle. But we would not know about his exceptional routine had people not observed and assisted it at every point.

The sense of society looking over the writer's shoulder could not have conduced to verve and originality. Pliny the Younger makes it clear that dutifulness was highest on his uncle's list; each morning he made the client's ceremonial call on the patron, in this case the emperor Vespasian; and the polymath spent a huge amount of time being read to and making excerpts – that is, transferring data from authoritative sources. The Romans found the readiest outlets for the resistant and creative self in short, occasional, and comic works, the sort of thing fellow diners might hear with pleasure: lyric poetry (including bawdy, invective, and love poetry), satire, and epigram.

How would someone like Vergil have managed to transform epic poetry in this society? The blanks in his biography and the emphasis on his personal elusiveness may indicate that his lifestyle was to a large degree invented, one that his associates found hard to understand, much less report on.

Horace's "Journey to Brundisium" satire, with its rare depiction of Vergil as a self-sacrificing client, on a strenuous trip to meet his patron at an important conference, is set quite early, in 40 BCE, before Octavian had even consolidated power, and before Vergil had delivered a single completed work that we know about. Later, as an established celebrity, could he come and go more or less as he wished? He had at least the use of residences in Sicily, a far and inconvenient distance from Rome. If he moved frequently between houses as a guest, he was probably fleeing distracting attentions.

"The Journey to Brundisium" may be helpful here as a *satirical* poem, going beyond the more conventional accounts—grateful, delighted—of hospitality and zeroing in on some of the burdens of the recipient. Along the route to the coast, demonstrative receptions are not hard to come by, but good taste, restraint, and a sense of the guests' real needs are. A long fragment of the Neronian-era *Satyricon* known as "Trimalchio's Dinner Party" shows the young educated guests in agonies of irritation at their freedman host's clumsy, nightlong efforts to impress them. They can run away at an opportune moment because he has not even registered who they are—but this was not the position of a poet attached to the imperial court.

The basic troublesome fact was that most Romans could not have understood why a man might want to be alone, particularly when a luxurious hoopla was going on in the dining room, and they would have laid concerned siege to a guest who shut himself in his room. The iconic solitary remained Timon of Athens, whom Aristophanes calls "an offshoot of the Furies" (*Lysistrata* 811), those hideous spirits of violent vengeance; a loner must be insane and need help.

Horace's rhetorical strategy in the face of excessive social demands (besides depicting himself in *Satires* 1.9 as trying one polite brush-off after another on a pesky fan) was to portray modest domestic and social comforts enjoyed with exquisite people; he thus conveyed that he was already keeping the company that could best help him contribute to his nation's culture, and so other people should leave him alone. As much sociability as would be useful to him professionally may have been part of Horace's modus operandi, but it does not seem like something Vergil would have found congenial. Virtuoso that he was, Horace could have written as much as he needed to — and at fewer than five hundred lines, *The Art of Poetry* is his longest poem — in his spare time.

When I was casting around as to how Vergil might have coped, it occurred to me that one excuse always seems to work to afford writers and intellectuals privacy and free time: poor health. Vergil is supposed to have been chronically ill. Though Romans prized officious public and social busyness, or "non-leisure," they also excused "respectable leisure," especially when its practitioner was sickly. Cicero (one of the busiest of them all) approved of his closest friend, the valetudinarian Atticus, staying out of public life though he was a wealthy, cultivated man from a prominent family. Atticus was an accomplished scholar, writer, and publisher, and Cicero's hyper-sympathetic letters suggest how his correspondent finessed a lifestyle in which he could do whatever he wanted, maintaining both control of his time and access to as much of the outside world as was convenient: he kept everyone around him worried that too much pressure would extinguish him. A writer did not need to be a plutocratic aristocrat to present such a scenario. Horace writes to Maecenas from his farm (a gift from Maecenas) that he is not ill but afraid of becoming ill if he travels, so his friend will of course pardon his staying put (*Epistles* 1.7.2–9).

A theory of psychosomatic illness was many centuries in the future. No one speculated that some people might have a more complicated relationship with their own health than the merely organic or the supernaturally influenced. Was Vergil one of these people, and perhaps the first of the important authors who throughout their careers carved out a place for themselves by making their bodies' frailties an excuse? Suetonius writes that although Vergil was a big, swarthy man, with a rustic appearance, "his health was up and down; he was very frequently subject to ailments of the stomach and throat and to headaches, and often vomited blood. He was very sparing in his consumption of food and wine" (Life 8–9).

Horace is a contemporary witness to his friend's digestive troubles (*Satires* 1.5.49), but acid reflux must have been common among Roman upper-class men, who ate dinners of many courses while lying down. Most of the ailments Suetonius lists are suggestively short of outward manifestations such as fevers, rashes, and impaired movement; spitting up blood is one such manifestation, but it is episodic and does not always have an audience. Vergil may have only reported these crises and never thoroughly explored available treatments. All the symptoms may be part of one or more progressive conditions, but if so, this would not accord with Vergil's decision to start a long overseas journey during what then counted as an advanced age, his fifties.

I would not push my speculation any farther, but I offer for consideration the breathtaking variety, adaptability, and boldness of modern authors' use of ill health, organic and contrived and deliberately aggravated. Elizabeth Barrett Browning had a wide range of mysterious debilities, and her immobilization—starting in a quack clinic during early adolescence—allowed her to study ancient languages like her envied brothers and read and write as much as she chose, instead of spending entire mornings on social visits, a duty commonly imposed on upper-class young girls with a view toward marrying them off: besides a controlling widowed father, she had her poor health standing between her and any marriage that did not comport with her literary ambitions. Charles Darwin's reported medical history might seem enough to make *On the Origin of Species* and *The Descent of Man* literally unthinkable, but these meticulous yet highly original works benefited from his rural isolation and his family's reverent care of him: a valetudinarian's lifestyle turned out to be just the thing. Robert Louis Stevenson had severe respiratory ailments from childhood, and his parents' worry cast a sort of blanket of autonomy over his whole life. He did qualify as an attorney but instead of practicing undertook a series of brutally wearing adventures in foreign parts, adventures that further undermined his health. He eventually did much of his literary work from bed, with assistance. Proust was severely asthmatic, a condition that bought him considerable freedom to explore emotional and social worlds that interested him. Health reasons also justified his withdrawal to the bedroom where he wrote *À la recherche du temps perdu.* Virginia Woolf had her first psychotic episode in her teens after the death of her mother; during most of her life she appeared to be merely eccentric, but she derived substantial benefits as a writer from the family dictum that she was mad. Madness was (for example) among the few protections a married woman could have from unlimited childbearing, and after her marriage Woolf was deemed too unstable to have even one child. Mid-twentieth-century American writers who had mental breakdowns favored long stays at McLean Hospital in Massachusetts, which became mythologized as a place of self-discovery and artistic reemergence.

The examples are kaleidoscopically numerous and varied, but the persistent impression is that illness, "real" or not, can be adaptive for writers requiring a long, strenuous, and whimsical-looking apprenticeship for a goal that is too far-fetched for their social circles to countenance. Vergil's career, as an early proposition, would have sounded reasonable in terms of "Let me alone to study quietly in a pleasant place; if I exert myself in public and in society, I will die like my brothers." The career's real terms — "The first Roman emperor Augustus, who cultivates me (for his own purposes) as a sickly, shy author with an obscure background and a late-blooming, resistant talent, will in two thousand years be treated skeptically or cursorily, and will often be confused with Saint Augustine; I will be *Vergil*" — were absurd; they could begin to be realized only in the time and under the circumstances that bodily fragility cleared for them.

The strength of many writers' commitment to their vocation shows in their willingness, if not to consciously make themselves suffer and shorten their lives, then to maneuver with what in hindsight looks like a defiance purposeful and reckless at the same time. Katherine Mansfield did not deliberately contract gonorrhea or knowingly choose a doctor bad enough to render it untreatable and debilitating through invasive surgery. But the illness bought her everything essential to her as a writer: permanent exile, freedom, and care as an invalid, and a social (but not financial) break with her wealthy and stifling family.

A powerful, controlling establishment figure, usually a father, who needs to be put at a distance features in many of these stories. The great authority over Vergil's life was the ruler of the known world. It would make sense if, not only to eschew a more strenuous life early on but also to get more distance from that man later and more say over his schedule and the other conditions under which he worked, Vergil suffered more digestive pain and coughed up more blood, or made these symptoms more of an issue, than he would have otherwise.

CHAPTER SEVEN

An Abrupt and Disturbing Ending

The warm-weather sailing season (the time of choice for travel on the storm-prone Mediterranean) of 19 BCE was a turning point for both Augustus and Vergil. Augustus had spent more than a decade consolidating power but had not achieved anything like what the sixth book of the *Aeneid* (which he had already heard recited) trumpeted as the paramount Roman mission, to conquer to the ends of the world (that is, the known world) and establish a Roman regime everywhere. Other nations might excel in the arts and sciences,

But Romans, don't forget that world dominion
Is your great craft: peace, and then peaceful customs;
Sparing the conquered, striking down the haughty.

(851–853)

Still, the emperor had had considerable success in pushing out the empire's boundaries, reforming provincial administration, expanding trade, and improving relationships with foreign nations that remained independent and able to threaten Rome's security and prestige. In early fall of the year 19, he was returning from a lengthy tour of the East that probably had the air of a victory lap.

In Athens he met up with his most important poet, who accompanied him toward home but died on the way. Vergil had set off for a three-year tour of Greece and part of the Near East, during which time he would polish the *Aeneid,* which was complete in twelve books, except for the occasional unfinished line. Suetonius sets the situation out fairly blandly:

> When he was fifty-two years old and wanted to give the *Aeneid* its last polish, he resolved to withdraw to Greece and Asia, and devote three whole years exclusively to improving the poem, so that he would be free afterward to spend the rest of his life on philosophy only. But once he had started this trip and came upon Augustus in Athens, while the latter was on his way back to Rome from the East, Vergil made up his mind not to make off but actually to return together with him; during a tour of the neighboring town of Megara, however, when the sun was boiling hot, he became ill and made his ailment worse by not putting off his voyage; hence when he landed at Brundisium he was substantially worse and within a few days died there, on the eleventh day before the Kalends of October [September 21]. (Life 35)

This outline in itself evokes some sharp suspicions. An elective three-year journey abroad, a proper tour that would have included many sites separated by seas and rough terrain, is an unusual choice for a man who purportedly had never been strong. Granted, Vergil would have enjoyed a well-appointed vessel and every amenity that was portable on land. But sea voyages were notoriously risky and unpleasant, and road travel was not much better. Mere bad local water, flea-infested bedding, or body lice after a period without the

customary daily bath could have produced the ailment that ultimately manifested and proved fatal to the poet. If we regard Vergil
merely as a tourist, his visit to Megara, which is a port trading city
without sites of great interest compared with those of Athens,
would speak to a desire for comprehensive sightseeing at considerable physical strain.

Travel as a means, or merely an occasion, to finish the *Aeneid* is
more suspicious still. The epic was probably close to its present
state of completion when he set off, since at his normal rate of work
he could not have done much to further it during the short time
before his death, and the posthumous editing of the poem before
its release was reportedly quite light. What did Vergil really still
need to do for the poem? Improving it may have become a sort of
addiction for him, but any rational person would have declared
what was already there superb and told him that it does not take
three years to fill out fifty-eight incomplete lines.

A journey also meant conditions far from ideal for work. For
example, as Cicero had found, if a writer himself stayed healthy
during his travels, a crucial assistant might still be afflicted and
have to be left behind. In addition, a library of scrolls carried along
as inspiration and reference material would have been bulky and
at risk from the elements. True, adventurous travel could have literary functions; for instance, Herodotus claims to have based his
accounts of foreign lands and cultures in the *Histories* on actual
visits and interviews, and Strabo drew on firsthand observation for
some of his *Geography*.

But that Vergil needed "local color" (as one reference work phrases
it) to put the finishing touches on the fictional *Aeneid* seems a far-
fetched, anachronistic notion. To make the settings of his epic poem
conform more exactly to the real places, and to devote three years
of hardships and dangers to doing so is not a project I can conceive

an ancient poet honestly undertaking. I know of no evidence that he dealt in this (for his time) strange way with his imaginative work, instead of being preoccupied with formal effects and the adaptation of the literary tradition, in which he was like other poets, only more intense in his efforts. Would he really have planned to take apart satisfactory lines in order, say, to place a grove more accurately above a bay in one of the *Aeneid*'s landscape descriptions?

And what about the plan to pursue philosophy for the rest of his life? Did he mean to retire abroad to do so? That would have been odd, as there were plenty of Greek sages in Italy, and he had the means to import others at his convenience. And did he plan to study philosophy alone, rather than with a conversational circle? That was hardly the usual proceeding — but of course Vergil was not bound by other people's practice. Or could he have imagined assembling a congenial group — like the one at Naples in his youth — while he was abroad? Did he mean to retire in Athens, among the young Roman students?

Finally, the trip seems a little like an imitation of Augustus' tour of the East, begun in the year 22. The emperor's rationale was obvious and indisputable: he wished to inspect important and extensive territories with a view to governing them more effectively. He probably would not have been impressed by any rationale Vergil could have offered him for a trip of a similar duration and a somewhat similar extent. Vergil may have asked to go along with his chief patron and been refused, in which case his resolve to travel on his own could have looked downright rebellious.

But even the tactfully worded version of his plans passed down to us suggests that he showed enough independence of mind to put his relationship with Augustus at risk. According to Suetonius, Vergil did not say he *needed* to travel in order to finish the *Aeneid*, or that he had much work left to do; he may have meant no more than that it would be three years before he declared the *Aeneid* finished. And "philosophy" could, as he had found years earlier, be a gloss for a pleasant, social retirement from public and professional activity. Whatever his specific philosophical interests at this point, he was in effect stipulating that he would write no more poetry under his patronage arrangements after the *Aeneid* was finished — or perhaps he would write no more poetry at all. Some writers, like Shakespeare and Rimbaud, leave literature, in some cases helped by a change of scene to a place that carries no expectations that their career will continue. At the least, in locations more remote than Sicily, his sometime retreat, Vergil could have expected better relief from the burdens of success as well as from the ordinary burdens of elite Roman life: the drawn-out social rituals, the ebullient affability and communicativeness, the crowds of attendants, with other people's staff added to one's own.

The elation of a departure overseas, away from the slough of personal attachment and expectation, and away from the ties of dedication to someone else's nation-building, is the happy climax of book 4 of the *Aeneid*, counterbalancing Dido's horrifying death caused by her reliance on a human relationship. It takes only the first 164 portentous lines of the book to build up to the love affair, whose beginning is described with 7 lines about horror, dire fate, dishonesty, and shame. The rest of the book, almost 550 lines, is devoted to the affair's consequences, starting with humiliating and dangerous rumors. When the cease-and-desist and marching orders arrive from Jove via Mercury, Aeneas is dressed up richly in his ruler-lover's gifts and directing her building projects (259–264): he is a metaphorical prostitute. He effectively sneaks away from her, his preparations happening in the background of bitter arguments over his obligations. Mercury speeds up the departure with a second, more urgent message, telling him that the crazed queen is about to destroy the fleet (556–570). The hero knows he is headed toward hardship, conflict, grief, and his own premature death, but he embraces his true fate in the moment of rejecting a false claimant to himself. That self is his only lasting vessel of hope and purpose. This hyper-dramatized fantasy could apply to Vergil's erotic life, as I discussed in Chapter 5. But I think that Dido's identity as a queen—bad-tempered, demanding, manipulative, and controlling in proportion to the extent that her position is new, insecure, and won at a terrible cost—points to Vergil's relationship to Augustus as well.

Vergil may not have announced his departure beyond his own retainers and a few others. I cannot believe that he had ever discussed it amicably with Augustus, who would have been anxious to keep him safe and steadily working until his great poem was complete and polished, and who would have been embarrassed at the prospect of the most famous poet of Italy and Rome abandoning both. (Consulting Maecenas might have been another matter; some relationship apparently remained: Suetonius writes that Vergil willed him a twelfth part of his estate [Life 37].) Maybe news of the decision started off overseas toward Augustus timeously but in a letter calculated to take weeks to reach him.

Various scenarios are arguable, but a few parameters emerge. The arrangements Vergil made with Varius before the departure about the disposition of his writings (Suetonius, Life 39) suggest that the trip was no secret, and indeed a traveler in the ancient world could not sneak away without resembling a runaway slave. He could not hide his proper entourage and substantial equipment, and if he went without them he would be wildly unsafe. But Augustus' absence on his long, distant mission at this period may have been a chance for Vergil to make a break for it, leaving without the emperor's knowledge or permission.

An Abrupt and Disturbing Ending

That Vergil merely "came upon" Augustus in Athens – the Latin verb indicates a chance meeting – beggars belief. By this point, Augustus must have known where Vergil was and may have dispatched an advance team to intercept him. In any case, the encounter would have been a tense one. Augustus' words and demeanor do not appear in Suetonius, but it is hard to conceive that Vergil's decision to give up so early on such momentous plans had no prompting behind it, and the language of faithfulness is stressed in the phrasing of his decision. The verb *absisto* means "make off" rather than simply "leave," and can be used for a personal or a military desertion: for some reason, the poet resolves not to abandon the emperor after all. And *etiam una,* "actually . . . together with," signals that Vergil did not return to Italy by his own route or in his own time or with an independent mobile household, but in the emperor's own company. It was a public display of unity. This throws into question Suetonius' indication that Vergil made his condition worse by not delaying the voyage. Certainly if the poet were to travel with the emperor, the date of departure would not be up to the poet.

Everything points to a fraught situation. Vergil might already, after years of negotiated settlements about the delivery schedule for *Aeneid* portions and revisions in the name of making the work as good as possible, have been looking at the end of Augustus' patience, comity, and flexibility; the emperor might have calculated that he could now crack down at little risk. After all, that weighty bargaining chip, the unfinished *Aeneid,* was as good as finished, and though the story of Vergil's deathbed treats the manuscript as unique and vulnerable, I cannot imagine that the emperor had not secured copies of the poem at several late stages of its composition. And despite his outward geniality and good humor, Augustus could be brutal, even – or especially – to those close to him; he ordered his newborn great-granddaughter exposed when her mother was in exile and disgrace, for example.

Perhaps the strongest hint that he now unfettered his annoyance lurks in the story that Vergil died of heatstroke. The decision to tour Megara — a port city important for trade, and hence of more natural interest to Augustus than to Vergil — in the blazing heat of early fall is curious, as would be the frail poet's overexposure to the sun at any time or place. If the Romans knew anything, it was how to deal with hot climates. In ordinary circumstances, including the hardships and inconveniences of travel, Vergil would not have contracted heatstroke by accident; the consequences would have been unspeakable for the slaves and other subordinates responsible for looking after him.

Did Augustus, alive to the difficulties of either controlling or sidelining the popular, well-liked author who had written the great national poem but then fled the nation, turn his mind to the advantages of Vergil's bad health worsening to a lethal degree? Did he have Vergil hiking around Megara at midday, or lingering unsheltered during the visit? Or is the story of Megara a cover for Augustus' keeping Vergil waiting in a treeless courtyard for an interview? At any rate, sunstroke has easy and intuitive treatments (water, rest, cooling), effective if they are applied immediately; if not, organ damage can be fatal. Was treatment of Vergil's condition withheld? Or was sunstroke a cover story for something else? Was there something in Vergil's refreshments?

Perhaps the poet himself, dressed down, threatened, and foreseeing a diminished life, committed virtual suicide in a handy but discreet way, simply by sending his litter away or refusing a drink or a dip in cool water. He might also have eaten or drunk something lethal: suicide had long been the standard way out for elite Romans checkmated in power struggles; they customarily sanctified the act by reference to philosophical ideals. Or perhaps Vergil intended only to make himself sick in order to be left behind when Augustus sailed. Letters of Cicero (see especially *Letters to Friends* 16.5) show the kind of civilized example set in the past: a man did not cause his valued dependent to travel when he was ill, no matter how much he needed or wanted him present.

In short, many less strange things could have happened than for the heat to afflict a privileged Roman so badly that he died some days later. I would not push my own speculative reconstruction of events; in fact, I invite others to try their hand at historical sleuthing, as they might do better. I insist only that the account in the ancient biographies sends discordant noises down the centuries.

Suetonius sets up the scene of Vergil's death in Brundisium from the time before the journey abroad begins. "Before leaving Italy, Vergil had tried to make Varius agree to incinerate the *Aeneid* if anything happened to him; Varius, however, had stubbornly refused to do it" (Life 39). If the conversation happened, it revealed a troubled, unrealistic mindset on Vergil's part. Did the poet really think that Varius would pledge himself to destroying a work so important to the regime? At any rate, it would have been understandable for Vergil to give Varius a copy of the up-to-date *Aeneid* for safekeeping, so maybe this was the basis for their meeting. Whatever was discussed, agreed, or left unsettled, the deathbed contest of wills over the fate of the poem seems too bizarre and disturbing to be a mere fiction. If it is one, what is it doing capping the biography of a generally sweet-natured, highly esteemed man?

The episode is illuminating even apart from Vergil, figuring as it does in the remote background to intellectual property rights. The ancients did believe that an author was entitled to the credit for what he had written; Vergil himself was accused of stealing

Homer's work. But the exclusive legal right to own and control creations of one's own mind appeared nowhere on the horizon; nothing, for example, prevented independent copyists and booksellers from treating a literary work as their own property and profiting from it. But authors' control over their work in progress was relatively straightforward inasmuch as periods of composition tended to be short and patronage (whether of individuals or of the state) not overtly or directly heavy-handed. It was as if societies went about their business with words and occasionally found themselves with literature on their hands — but nearly always by this point the author had signed off on it, if he was not dead as well.

A new kind of muddle manifested when Vergil became seriously ill with the *Aeneid* not quite finished. His contemporaries recognized a real, embodied genius, with an untold capacity for expressiveness, and thus with an untold power that his chief sponsor might share; powerful as this man was, his poet could enhance his power — but because of the poet's virtual fusion with his unfinished work, his death represented a crisis instead of a simple bequeathing.

As Augustus was an artist of power himself, he could not leave Vergil alone and had probably been pushing and negotiating for a long time concerning such issues as the amount of regime-promotional material necessary in the poem, how subtle the material should be, and how quality and speed of production should balance out. In addition, members of the emperor's circle had competed with the author (amateur competitors figure obtrusively in the *Eclogues*) and micromanaged him (how could the poet-politicos have been kept out of Vergil's critique sessions?), no doubt on the theory that they must be experts on anything important that was taking form. Vergil was fed up and more than ready to assert that this was *his* work. But he was not practiced in confrontation, and those around him were not used to it.

Typical of his complaisance was his initial reading of at least three books of the *Aeneid* aloud to Augustus before they were finished. At this early stage, their text can hardly have been more complete and more polished than the one we inherited, which contains a number of incomplete lines. But a work was effectively published by being performed, on which occasion any patron would of course receive a copy. Augustus had at least a quarter of the epic in his hands, and he might well not have perceived much difference in the quality of any further part of it he saw. Some early episodes are inherently more exciting (man-eating monsters and romance help), but Vergil was not a mere storyteller. He was an incomparable developer of Latin poetry's music and intellectual suggestiveness; in my view as his translator, even a mustering scene of his — that is, a long account of what various troops looked like and where they came from — is a mass of ingenuity, if for no other reasons than that he felt compelled to keep his standards up while composing it and that by the time he came to this Iliadic challenge, he had added years to his experience. In short, the parts of the *Aeneid* written later are bound to hold special interest and show a special kind of refinement, and Vergil knew it, even if Augustus did not.

Had Vergil worked on the poem so single-mindedly and devotedly and for so long that he now insisted, and really thought, that the entire manuscript was still the sacrosanct vehicle of his ongoing intentions? He may have mentally placed it in the contemporary category of a will or other legal document, which could be left secure and inviolable in a temple until after its author's death. "Deposit" was a category of Roman law and custom that also applied between individuals: formally leaving an object with a friend did not in itself diminish ownership of that object. Was that what Vergil had in mind when he gave Varius an *Aeneid* manuscript, if he did? Was he handing over the object but mentally reserving his rights? The term "literary executor" that some modern scholars apply to Varius is not as far-fetched as it seems at first if Vergil were, in effect, anticipating a world in which his wishes could control his written words after his death, even to the point of having the words destroyed. In his case, the wishes were a testimony to authorship as a sort of humble transcendence.

His attitude anticipated modern controversies over literary rights. But as prophetic as Vergil was, he was also off his head. He shows no awareness that Varius could not fail to represent Augustus' interests. Any relevant manuscript that Varius knew the existence of could not escape copying for the emperor. Moreover, Vergil had assistants with detailed knowledge of and privileged access to his papers, who knew which side their bread was ultimately buttered on. It is even questionable who such people functionally belonged to: if patrons could supply catamites to Vergil, they could also supply secretaries and scholarly assistants whose loyalty would remain at their powerful source, and who could never be too far from Rome to report back.

If we need to speak of Vergil's politics (stretching that term about as far as it will go), this fishbowl is a much sounder explanation than ideological disagreement with the regime for the *Aeneid*'s famous theme of uncontrollable rage, or *furor*. In the poem, furor may figure as something within the forces of nature (such as bad weather and animals fighting), women out of control, warriors – including Aeneas toward and at the end – set on vengeful destruction, and supernatural beings who incite insane violence. The amount of harm a vicious and self-indulgent universe inflicts to frustrate the hero is wildly far-fetched, but it is not at all far-fetched that in the poem's last lines he should lash back with violence weighed and rationalized on the spot, murdering the surrendered, suppliant Turnus and explaining to him why. The other actors have been full of natural furor or infused with it by some force beyond their control. But Aeneas never needed a god or demon to poison or goad him. Furor becomes part of his personality through day-to-day experience; and the assimilation is, at least at this last moment, conscious and willed.

The story of Aeneas' arrival at this juncture is cogent. For example, the episode of the Trojan refugees' settlement on Crete in book 3 has an exasperated but helpless feel. Aeneas' father, Anchises, interprets a prophecy to mean that Crete is their goal, but a year of building, farming, administrative set-up, and the formation of young families ends in a devastating plague and a "Whoops, silly me! It's *Italy* the prophecy meant!" from Anchises, whose godlike paternal authority is not backed up by any intellectual prowess. What did Vergil have to put up with from the court, and what did it do to him inwardly? Were Augustus' summonses ever capricious? Was Vergil sometimes stood up after responding to them? Did the emperor, in his pretentions to critical astuteness, ever prod Vergil into (secret) fury by interfering directly with his writing?

Whatever the cause, there was a blow-up at Vergil's deathbed. Perhaps Varius' refusal to destroy the *Aeneid* manuscript belongs to this scene and not to the conversation in Italy prior to Vergil's journey: that would better explain the connecting word I translate as "therefore." "Therefore as his illness reached its crisis, Vergil would not stop demanding his scroll cases, meaning to burn them himself; but since no one brought them, he gave no detailed testamentary instructions about [the *Aeneid*]. Yet he bequeathed the same Varius, and also Tucca, his writings on the condition that they publish nothing that had not been [or "would not have been"] published by himself. However, under Augustus' authority, Varius published it with only cursory edits, actually leaving the incomplete lines as they were" (Life 39–41).

Whatever manuscript this was—possibly the sole manuscript that could have transmitted the *Aeneid* as we have it?—there was no chance that Vergil could have gotten at it from the bed where his last strength was leaving him. Was he woozy enough to think that someone would hand him an armful of scroll cases along with a flint and some kindling for making a fire on the bedding or the floor? But it is even less credible that practically in the next moment, and in a complete change of mood, he retreated from giving any specific instructions about the poem, and then, practically in the *next* moment, bequeathed his oeuvre to the very two people Augustus would have wanted in charge of it, and on a condition they could either adhere to or ignore: that nothing be released that the author had not released himself. The Latin could also mean that a given part of the bequeathed oeuvre *would not have been published by himself*—so Varius and Tucca could invent or reinvent his judgment and wishes. Even granted the more objective use of the subjunctive mood, the verb "released" or "published" could mean that he had read it (or part of it) at the court or that a written version had come into the emperor's hands—which was not something over which the poet necessarily had any control. But maybe the narrative has been misted over on purpose, with the confusion obscuring an embarrassing core reality: Vergil turned violently against his work and did not pass beyond that mood before he died, or he turned against the people who had fostered his work, decreeing that they did not deserve it.

In any event, with Augustus' go-ahead, the *Aeneid* was published in nearly the exact state in which Vergil had left it. Perhaps poems in what we call the *Appendix Vergiliana* were counted as unpublished and held back, and this was the distinction honored; but if so, these poems got out eventually. But none of the posthumous arrangements, however pragmatic or well intentioned, could blot out the reality that Vergil's life — like the *Aeneid* itself — ended in a blaze of rage, and that those around him merely shuffled through both endings, ignoring their heat.

I contrast the death of Turnus and Vergil's own demands at his death with his purported epitaph at Naples, where Suetonius reports his bones were interred (Life 36). "Mantua gave birth to me, the Calabrians [Brundisium counted as a Calabrian city at the time] snatched me away; / Now Parthenope [Naples] holds me: I sang pastures, fields, chieftains." It is most likely not Vergil's own couplet. But its content is interesting. Notice how places act forcibly, even violently on the speaker, one giving birth to him only for the inhabitants of the city he died in to "snatch away/capture/plunder" him. His adoptive city now "holds/grips/owns" him. He is active only in the second half of the second verse, and only in singing, but he sings comprehensively, acting with his voice alone on much larger places, those in which farming takes place, and then on leaders of the second greatest undertaking of the ancient world, war. The fragile, defenseless person is the ultimate lord of these strenuous, risky, and all-important enterprises.

"Vergil" literally has the last word about having the last word. It is an ironic testimony, personal sounding but probably not from the author, about an individual who found ways to use his limitations to give his imaginary art a new reach into the limitless.

Chronology

All dates BCE unless otherwise specified.

91–87	Social War between Rome and its Italian allies
88	Sulla marches on Rome and assumes the dictatorship
87–86	Marius marches on and occupies Rome
70	Vergil born on October 15
58–50	Caesar wages a series of successful military campaigns in Gaul
55	Vergil assumes the toga of manhood
ca. 49	Vergil's education completed, he moves to Naples
49	Caesar invades Italy, beginning a new round of civil wars
43	Cicero assassinated on December 7
44	Caesar assassinated on March 15
42	Caesar's republican assassins and their allies defeated at the Battle of Philippi
39–38	Vergil's *Eclogues* completed, *Georgics* begun
31	Octavian defeats Antony and Cleopatra in the Battle of Actium
30	Vergil's *Georgics* completed, *Aeneid* begun
27	Octavian is granted the title Augustus
23	Augustus gains complete control of the Senate
20	Recovery of the Roman standards from the Parthians
19	Vergil departs Italy for an extended period abroad in the summer
	Death of Vergil, September 21
17	Augustus revives the Secular Games
8 CE	Exile of the poet Ovid
14 CE	Death of Augustus

Source Notes

All translations of ancient literature that appear in this book are my own, and include excerpts from my translation of *Aeneid: Vergil,* rev. ed., edited by Susanna Braund (New Haven: Yale University Press, 2021).

INTRODUCTION

Extant biographies of Vergil start with Suetonius, who wrote more than a hundred years after the poet's death but probably had access to an account by Vergil's close associate Varius. Accounts expanded and became more fanciful in Late Antiquity; I have generally stuck to Suetonius, only tentatively citing a little information that appeared later. Suetonius also writes of the lives of Vergil's contemporary poets Horace and Tibullus, and these and other literary biographies are available in English in Suetonius, *Lives of the Caesars,* vol. 2: *Claudius. Nero. Galba, Otho, Vitellius. Vespasian, Titus, Domitian. Lives of Illustrious Men: Grammarians and Rhetoricians. Poets (Terence. Virgil. Horace. Tibullus. Persius. Lucan). Lives of Pliny the Elder, Passienus Crispus,* rev. ed. trans. J. C. Rolfe, Loeb Classical Library 38 (Cambridge: Harvard University Press, 1997).

I do not cite biographical works on modern authors unless these works contain new research or other unique assertions on which I rely. In my introduction I have singled out Hermione Lee, *Virginia Woolf's Nose: Essays on Biography* (Princeton: Princeton University Press, 2005); Stephen Greenblatt, *Will in the World: How Shakespeare Became Shakespeare,* rev. ed. (New York: Norton, 2016); and Heather Clark, *Red Comet: The Short Life and Blazing Art of Sylvia Plath* (New York: Knopf, 2020).

CHAPTER 1. ORIGINS

There are two previous modern book-length biographies of Vergil: Frank Tenney, *Vergil: A Biography* (New York: Holt, 1922), and Peter Levi, *Virgil: His Life and Times* (New York: St. Martin's, 1998). Caesar's own account of the late Roman civil wars, supplemented by accounts written in his name, is almost exclusively an overseas military history and of little interest for a life of Vergil. The most comprehensive ancient account of the period is by a Greek historian named Appian, who wrote in the second century CE. A translation can be found in *Appian's Roman History,* vol. 4, *The Civil Wars, Books 3.27–5,* trans. Horace White, Loeb Classical Library 5 (London: William Heinemann, 1913). I have found two modern autobiographical works particularly valuable for thinking about the childhoods of great authors: Lev Tolstoy's writings pub-

Source Notes

lished in English as *Childhood, Boyhood, Youth,* trans. Judson Rosengrant (New York: Penguin, 2012); and J. M. Coetzee, *Boyhood: Scenes from Provincial Life* (London: Secker and Warburg, 1997).

CHAPTER 2. THREE KINDS OF LITERARY EDUCATION

The ancient sources on education are voluminous and very detailed. I recommend Mark Joyal, Iain McDougall, and J. C. Yardley, *Greek and Roman Education: A Sourcebook* (New York: Routledge, 2009), which draws from a variety of these sources.

CHAPTER 3. LITERARY EXPERIMENTS AND THE LITERARY LIFESPAN

The *Appendix Vergiliana* is notoriously garbled and difficult. I have relied on the text and translation in *Vergil*, vol. 2: *Aeneid, Books 7–12. Appendix Vergiliana,* trans. H. R. Fairclough, rev. G. P. Goold, Loeb Classical Library 64, 3rd ed. (Cambridge: Harvard University Press, 2000). The quotations appear on pp. 371–372. I found a useful summary of the scholarship on the difficult issues of authenticity in Scott McGill's "The *Appendix Vergiliana,*" in the *Cambridge Companion to Virgil* (Cambridge: Cambridge University Press, 2019), 63–76.

CHAPTER 4. PATRONAGE

The first Loeb volume of Suetonius includes an important life of Augustus on which I drew for this chapter: Suetonius, *Lives of the Caesars,* vol 1: *Julius, Augustus, Tiberius, Gaius Caligula,* 3rd ed., trans. J. C. Rolfe, Loeb Classical Library 31 (Cambridge: Harvard University Press, 1998).

CHAPTER 5. LOVE AND ART

Amy Richlin's *The Garden of Priapus: Sexuality and Aggression in Roman Humor,* rev. ed. (New York: Oxford University Press, 1992), helps to contextualize Vergil's erotic experiences and feelings.

CHAPTER 6. THE WORK TAKES OVER

An accessible classic that sheds a broad light on Vergil's development of the hexameter is L. R. Palmer's *The Latin Language* (London: Faber and Faber: 1954). A number of histories of Latin literature explain in general terms his culminating achievements as an epic poet; my personal favorite is *The Cambridge History of Classical Literature,* vol. 2: *Latin Literature,* ed. E. J. Kenney and W. V Clausen (Cambridge: Cambridge University Press, 1982).

Source Notes

CHAPTER 7. AN ABRUPT AND DISTURBING ENDING

Hermann Broch's *The Death of Virgil* (New York: Pantheon, 1945) is a novel by a refugee from the Third Reich that depicts Vergil as an antitotalitarian Christ figure, with a lost female lover haunting the last hours of his meditations. My excuse for my own speculative flights concerning Vergil's death is the same one Broch could have adduced for his: the most important author of the ancient world draws meaning to himself like a magnet. Another important novelization is Ursula K. Le Guin's *Lavinia* (New York: Harcourt, 2008). In this story, the silent princess Lavinia of the *Aeneid* acquires a voice.

Index

Index

Index

Index

Index

Index

Varro, 19

Varus, Alfenus, 21

Vatinius, Publius, 62

Venus, 55; as Aeneas' mother, 31, 131–132

Vergil: and ability to remain in Augustus' favor, 95–100; activist readings of, 6; Alexandrians as influence on and source for, 58–59, 128; and Augustus, 53–54, 83–84, 86–90; avoidance of busy life, 148–149; background and environment of, 6–7, 13–14; beekeeping as interest of, 24–26; and a biographer's challenges in telling his life story, 1–6; and the challenge of hexameter, 144–145; challenges faced by, late in his career, 103–107; characters in poetry of, 41–42; childhood and youth as ideals in the work of, 89–90; on classroom discipline, 50; criticism of, by his contemporaries, 43–44; as Dante's guide in the *Inferno* and the *Purgatorio*, 5; death of, 156–157, 163, 167, 169; early exposure to poor and powerless people as influence on, 35–37; early impressions of, 43; education of, 17, 45, 46–47, 50, 51; ethnic background of, 15–16; explicit language as used by, 113; family background of, 11–12, 18, 22; farming as part of his early background, 23–27; as first modern author, 8–9, 50; and friendships from his school days, 53; full name of, 11, 15; half-brother of, 30; health problems experienced by, 151–152, 154; as Horace's friend and supporter, 79; literary friendships of, 60–63, 140; as lover of the coun-

tryside, 38; Lucretius as influence on, 55; methodologies of, when composing, 138–139; philosophy as alluded to in his work, 54–56, 159; as prominent figure in ancient Rome, 81–82; questions surrounding the death of, 156–58, 161–163, 167–168; as resident of Naples, 13, 53–54, 56–57; sexuality of, 34–35, 56, 109–110, 111–112, 125; as sexually timid, 113; siblings of, 29; and slow manner of speaking, 43, 48; social position of, 22–23, 27–29; as student of Greek, 44; and stylistic similarities to the work of Maecenas, 116–119; and suffering related to erotic feelings, 119–120, 129; and time required for composing poetry, 135–140, 147–148; on tour in Greece and the Near East, 156, 158; as valuable to Augustus, 100. See also *Aeneid; Appendix Vergiliana; Eclogues; Georgics*

Vespasian, Emperor, 149

Vesuvius, Mount, 57

Vipsanius, Marcus, 118, 119

White, E. B., 64

women, Roman: allure of, associated with suffering, 124–125; role of, in Vergil's time, 29–32

Woolf, Virginia, 153

Xenophon, 5

Yeats, W. B., "Sailing to Byzantium," 129

Zeus, 32

Zoilus of Amphipolis, 119